COLLINS

everyday
scots
LAW

GEORGE WAY

D0995819

HarperCollins*Publishers*

HarperCollins Publishers
Westerhill Rd, Bishopbriggs, Glasgow G64 2QT

www.**fire**and**water**.com

First published 2000

© George Way 2000

Reprint 10 9 8 7 6 5 4 3 2 1 0

ISBN 0 00 472493 3

A catalogue record for this book is available from The British Library

George Way asserts his moral right to be identified as the author of this work

Printed in Great Britain by
Caledonian International Book Manufacturing Ltd, Glasgow

Contents

Dedication

This work is dedicated to the memory of the late Professor W.A. (Bill) Wilson who, despite his awesome erudition, taught his students at the Faculty of Law of the University of Edinburgh (now known, less grandly, as the Edinburgh Law School) that the holder in due course of an endorsed bill of exchange (*Jock hoping to cash Jimmys' cheque given to him by Rab to settle a debt*) can equally be called 'the sucker'.

Introduction

Heu, moda itera omnia quae mihi nunc
nuper narravisti, sed nunc Anglice?
Listen, would you repeat all that, but this time in English?

The use of technical terms can rarely be avoided in any walk of life: they have the legitimate purpose of conveying detail in a shorthand way to someone similarly trained which would otherwise need to be done at some length. Anyone who has seen a camel knows what it looks like, but try describing one to the proverbial visitor from another planet. Legal jargon is no different and is, quite properly, used by lawyers to conjure up in the minds of other lawyers the principles, facts and cases they learned in law school which lie behind the Latin maxims or convoluted English. This book seeks to explain some of the major areas where the law impacts on our daily lives and to guide the reader through the maze of legal concepts and jargon which otherwise might appear obscure or just downright incomprehensible.

We generally only think about our legal rights and obligations when something has gone wrong. While this work may be a first port of call or an aid to understanding, it is not a substitute for proper legal advice which you should seek at the earliest opportunity to resolve your problem.

I must thank all those at Beveridge & Kellas who helped with this project, and in particular my partner, Lynn Harrison SSC, who contributed her particular expertise on marriage, children, divorce and the impact of these areas on tenancy and land law; Ruth Hinsley, solicitor, who compiled the glossary for me to translate; Teresina Valente, solicitor, who revised the chapter on rights at work and Gillian Conlon SSC. Olivia Storrie, Marie Hawthorn and Valerie MacInnes transformed my rough manuscript into pristine type through the witchcraft of modern word processing and put up with the endless revisions without serious complaint. While I acknowledge all support, the responsibility for any errors or omissions remains mine.

Finally, I must thank Jim Carney, Commissioning Editor at HarperCollins, for all his support. Having worked with me before on other books, he has already heard all my excuses for being behind schedule yet still has the courtesy to pretend he believes them.

George Way
Edinburgh 2000

The Author

George Way SBStJ, LL.B(hons), FRSA, FSA(Scot), NP, SSC.is a
native of Edinburgh and graduated in Law with Honours from the
University of Edinburgh in 1978. He was apprenticed to
Beveridge & Kellas SSC in Leith where he has been a litigation
partner since 1985. An accredited commercial mediator, he is a
council member of the Society of Solicitors in the Supreme Courts
and an external assessor to the California State Military Reserve
Court Martial Review Board.

A Fellow of the Royal Society of Arts and of the Society of
Antiquaries in Scotland, he has been the Honorary Secretary of
the Standing Council of Scottish Chiefs since 1982 and became a
Freeman of the City of Glasgow in 1997.

His other publications include the best selling *Collins Scottish
Clan and Family Encyclopedia* and *Homelands of the Clans*, both
published by HarperCollins.

Consumer Rights

The usual day-to-day activities of life often create legal rights and obligations about which most of us do not give a second thought unless something goes wrong. Every time we buy a newspaper, get on a bus or go out for a meal we are entering into a contract which has legal consequences.

The law of contract, as it has developed over the centuries, has always provided a basic framework to sort out disputes between parties but the late nineteenth and twentieth centuries saw the development of statutory law and codes forming what we now loosely call 'consumer law', which is designed to protect individuals from being misled by false claims, harmed by dangerous products or duped by incomprehensible or unreasonable 'small print' clauses.

The fundamental principle remains *caveat emptor* – let the buyer beware. This means that because it is the consumer who chooses the product or services they must use their own judgement. They are expected to know their own mind and take sensible precautions to ensure that what they are buying is what they want.

When things do go wrong you should complain quickly and in clear terms. You should put the complaint in writing, if necessary, and keep copies of all letters. All professionals and many tradesmen are members of associations or societies which have complaints procedures. There are also various organisations that have watchdogs called **Ombudsmen**, for example the insurance and banking industries. These individuals investigate complaints that the way in which your complaint has been handled was inadequate or unfair. There is no doubt that taking a complaint to court should always be the last resort but getting advice at an early stage is imperative. Solicitors and Citizens Advice Bureaux can help by advising you on the relevant law and the best way to claim effectively. Legal aid may be available to cover the costs of making such claims. You should also try contacting the trading standards department of your local authority which has powers to investigate certain types of complaint.

WHAT IS A CONTRACT?

Any agreement to obtain goods or services is a contract and it does not have to be in writing, nor even be verbal, in order to be valid. For example, when you get on a bus and pay the correct fare there is a contract between you and the bus company even though nothing has been said to indicate this. In consumer contracts there will be two parties with mutually enforceable rights and obligations.

Written contract

You will generally be legally bound by a written contract whether or not you have read it. For example, if you park your car in a private car park the ticket will often have terms and conditions on the back. You may not have read them or, having read them, may not agree with them, but they are part of your contract with the car park owner and define your rights. Similarly, if you sign a contract without reading it you are still bound by its terms unless you can prove that you were unable to read or were otherwise prevented from understanding it or you were misled by the other party about what it meant. You should always take the time to read a contract document and never sign one which contains blanks or is only partially completed.

A written contract may not, of course, reflect all the discussions which parties may have leading up to their agreement. For this reason many contracts contain a clause called an 'entire contract'. This provides that the document is to be considered as containing all the terms of the contract. You therefore cannot ask the court to consider any other negotiations or letters, etc. which you say may help to explain what the contract means. If there is no 'entire contract' clause then you would be able to lead evidence before a court that the written contract did not truly reflect the terms that had been agreed. An 'entire contract' clause can also be challenged if it was inserted into the contract unfairly or unreasonably.

CONTRACTUAL RIGHTS

Only the parties to a contract can rely on its terms. If you buy a microwave oven which does not work then you have contractual rights against the shop which sold it to you but if you give the microwave to someone as a wedding present then they have no rights at all against the shop because they were not a party to the original sale agreement. They could, however, ask you to take it back to the shop to enforce your obligations under the contract. The position is different if the microwave is actually dangerous as the recipient could make a complaint under the Consumer Protection Act 1987 (see Accidents, p. 54). There would also be a claim for any injury caused by negligence, whether you bought the microwave yourself or for another person who received it as a gift.

ARE ALL AGREEMENTS CONTRACTS?

There are many things we might agree to do for someone but which the law does not convert into contracts. An obvious example is where a friend agrees to give you a lift to the airport but oversleeps, so that you miss your plane. The incident might cause considerable bad feeling but you do not have the right to sue your friend for your loss. The position might be different if your friend ran a taxi business and was offering to do the trip for nothing. Scots law, unlike English law, states that a contract can be formed even though one party is obtaining some form of goods or services but is not paying for them. English law requires the concept of 'consideration' but this is alien to our legal system. The real difference is that the professional taxi driver is expected to know what he has undertaken by offering you a lift to the airport and therefore it does not matter whether he does this free of charge, whereas a friend acting in a private capacity does not take on this level of obligation.

Children under certain ages cannot be bound by what would otherwise be regarded as contractual obligations (see Children, p. 153).

STATUTORY RIGHTS

There is a whole raft of Acts of Parliament and regulations which apply to the sale of goods and the provision of services and it is perhaps useful, in the first instance, simply to list these. They are as follows:

- the Trade Descriptions Act 1968;

- the Supply of Goods (Implied Terms) Act 1973;

- the Consumer Credit Act 1974;

- the Unfair Contract Terms Act 1977;

- the Sale of Goods Act 1979;

- the Unfair Terms in Consumer Contracts Regulations 1999.

The main purpose of the legislation is to imply into contracts terms which are designed to protect the consumer. These **implied terms** relate to the nature of the contract itself and to the goods and services which are to be supplied. The law will always imply that goods which are sold will be similar to any sample which had been indicated by the seller. It also provides that existing provisions in a contract may be illegal if, for example, they seek to exclude liability for causing death or personal injury. There are a number of criminal sanctions which consumer law imposes but as these are all enforced through trading standards officers or the police it is unnecessary to discuss them at length here. Suffice it to say that, if concerned, you can report such matters to the authorities and where appropriate they will take action themselves.

UNFAIR TERMS

Regulations now exist which mean that businesses can no longer
rely on unfair terms in their contracts and that all terms must be
written in plain, understandable English. The regulations only
apply to terms in standard form contracts, for example the pre-
printed contracts which most of us will have seen when hiring a
car. The regulations provide that an unfair term is anything
contrary to the requirement of good faith which causes a
significant imbalance of the parties' rights, to the detriment of the
consumer. The term 'good faith' is very much related to the
bargaining strength between the parties. Contracts which are
presented on a 'take it or leave it' basis are the most likely to be
attacked by this legislation. The legislation is not free from
difficulty and there are provisions which seek to provide some
protection to the businessman:

- the regulations do not apply if the contractual terms have been
  negotiated for the individual transaction; Note: a term will
  always be deemed not to be individually negotiated if it is
  drafted in advance and therefore the consumer has had no real
  opportunity to influence its content.

- if the term is found to be unfair it is only that part of the
  contract which is cut down and if the rest of the contract still
  makes sense then that will be enforceable;

- not all contracts are covered, for example contracts of
  employment are specifically excluded;

- the requirements that the terms be in plain and understandable
  English do not affect some of the most important terms of a contract. For example, the price of goods cannot be set aside on the

ground of unfairness. This is for the self-evident reason that the law presumes that you knew what you were being charged and it is unreasonable for legislation to second guess parties' negotiations on this point. The general law of contract may, of course, still provide help here as there may be no contract at all if you were deceived as to the real cost you would be asked to pay.

DISCRIMINATION

The supplier of goods and services cannot discriminate against a prospective customer on the grounds of race, sex, marital status or disability. This applies across a whole range of activities including accommodation, banking, insurance, loans, credit facilities and transport, etc. The person who discriminates unlawfully can be sued for damages which would include *solatium* (see Glossary, p. 263).

IMPLIED TERMS RELATING TO GOODS

Quality

Goods must be of satisfactory quality and also fit for their normal purpose. These two conditions can overlap.

A central heating boiler which cuts out after an hour's use is neither of satisfactory quality nor fit for its purpose. However if you buy a computer with the express intention that it be used for high-quality photographic work it may be of satisfactory quality but if it lacks the video software to display your pictures then it is not fit for your purpose. This requirement also applies to cosmetic matters; unless something is expressly sold as being imperfect then it must be delivered in pristine condition and not dented or scratched. The 'satisfactory quality' test does incorporate the concept of reasonableness and therefore whether goods are acceptable must be decided with regard to their price, durability and the normal use to which such goods would be put. The question of normal use is important as, for example, you will not be able to complain about a saw designed for wood if you have been attempting to saw up concrete blocks. Goods will also be considered fit for their purpose if most consumers would be satisfied with them. If you were to purchase swimming goggles which kept out most of the water but were not effective to prevent your eyes from irritation because you have a specific chlorine allergy, you would not be able to reject them as being defective.

For these conditions to apply, the goods must also be sold in the course of trade, so that the legislation does not apply if, for example, you are buying a second-hand car from a friend.

Retailers cannot avoid their implied legal obligations by putting exemption clauses in the contract or by displaying notices such as 'No refunds or returns'. The fact that goods are bought for a reduced price during a sale is irrelevant. The position would be different if the goods were specifically sold as seconds and your attention was drawn to possible defects at the time of sale.

Sale by description

The goods must also be 'as described'. Goods are too often misdescribed. For example, a label on a packet may say 'sugar free' when in fact the product inside contains natural sugars and what the manufacturer means is that there has been no sugar added. There are cases which go the other way, of course. In one case a seller of 'T' shirts bearing the logos of companies such as Levi's, Adidas and Reebok was prosecuted for misdescription. He was acquitted of applying false trade descriptions because the goods were sold beside a notice saying 'brand copies'. The court was also influenced by the fact that the usual cost of the real branded items would have been £12–15 whereas these goods cost £1.99.

Title to goods

There is an implied term that the seller has the right to sell the goods to you. If you buy golf clubs at a car boot sale and they subsequently turn out to be stolen and are reclaimed by the owner, you are then entitled to a full refund from the seller.

DELIVERY

If you are not taking the goods with you at the point of purchase and the seller has agreed to deliver them he must do so within a reasonable time. You should be clear as to the agreement on delivery and if the date and time are crucial, make sure you get these in writing. A seller is not usually entitled to deliver in instalments unless you have agreed to this. If you have ordered a specially made three-piece suite you can refuse to accept delivery of the sofa on its own. Even if you agree to accept the sofa, the seller may still be in breach of contract if he does not promptly deliver the other chairs.

THE PRICE OF GOODS

Unless it was agreed at the time of purchase that the price could change, you are only obliged to pay the original cost. If the seller will not deliver the goods to you unless you meet some extra cost you can hold him to be in breach of contract and not only claim back any deposit you have paid but seek damages if you require to buy the goods elsewhere at a higher price. The position would be different if the contract provided that you were to pay for some element of the work based on the cost of materials at the time of manufacture. This might happen where you have ordered a particular covering for your sofa which is being re-built. The work may take several months and it would not be unusual for the upholsterer to stipulate that the cost of the material would be the prevailing cost at the time the work was done. You should, however, insist on a price guide and, if possible, that you are consulted on the actual price before the work commences. This would give you the option of settling for a cheaper material. Shops are entitled to charge more if you do not pay cash, for example by credit card, but they must display clear notification of this fact at the entrance to the shop and at the till or checkout.

Paying by credit card

If you have paid for goods by credit card but they are subsequently not delivered you will be able to claim a refund from the credit card company. The interest rates on credit cards may be unattractive but in this area they offer a distinct protection. If, for example, you pay £600 by cheque for a sofa and during the manufacturing process the factory is closed down you will not get a refund or even the sofa from any liquidator because he has to wind up the affairs of the business and share whatever is left with all the creditors, of which you are only one. However if you made the same payment by credit card you would be protected and guaranteed a refund from the credit card company.

REJECTING GOODS

If goods are totally unusable or unsatisfactory from the outset a customer is always entitled to a full refund. Retailers often tell customers to complain to the manufacturer about faulty merchandise. The purchaser's contract of sale is with the **retailer** and if you do not receive an adequate replacement from it then you are entitled to a full refund of the price. If you keep the goods for a period of time you may be said to have accepted the faulty goods, in which case you will lose the right to a replacement or a full refund. This will not happen until you have had a reasonable opportunity of examining the goods, and what is reasonable will depend on the type of product and all other circumstances. You must anticipate that if you keep the goods for a considerable length of time you are likely to be taken to have accepted them. If you do reject the goods promptly it is not your obligation to return them to the retailer. It is enough that you notify it of your rejection and the defects you have found. The retailer must then make arrangements to uplift the goods. You must act reasonably and not use the goods for any purpose while you are waiting for them to be collected.

If there is a manufacturer's guarantee this will give you additional rights to return the goods to the manufacturer but this is often unrealistic because it may well be at the other end of the country. This right does not prevent you from taking matters up directly with the retailer but may prove useful if the shop has gone out of business.

MAIL ORDER

The buyer of mail order goods has precisely the same rights as any other individual but, of course, it may be much harder to enforce those rights when you are not able to visit the seller's premises in person. It is certainly far more sensible to pay for mail order goods by credit card. You should keep copies of all advertisements, order forms and as many details as you can to prove what you were hoping to buy and from whom. There is a mail order traders' association and a Mail Order Protection Scheme which helps to deal with complaints about goods bought in this way.

HIRE PURCHASE

When you buy goods on hire purchase or other forms of conditional sale agreement, the supplier of the goods is not legally the seller. What is happening is that the supplier is selling the goods outright to the finance company which then enters into an agreement with you to let you use the goods in return for monthly payments. There are many different types of contract in this area: some where the goods will never belong to you and others where there is a payment at the end of the period of the hire contract by which you can acquire ownership. You do have contractual rights against the finance company but if your dispute relates to the fitness of the goods for the purpose you intended its position is likely to be that you used your skill and judgement in choosing the item you wanted and it merely purchased it at your request.

Generally speaking, you have the same rights in respect of hired goods as a buyer has but because the contractual relationships are more complicated it is not always easy to enforce them. You will have rights against the supplier of goods if you can show that you relied on representations by him as to the quality or fitness for purpose of the goods. You should be clear, however, that although internally the finance house and its dealer or supplier may have arranged matters so that the dealer or supplier will deal with your complaints about goods on a day-to-day basis, in law your rights are against the finance company. In the case of major consumer items such as cars the manufacturer may agree to bear some responsibility for repairs, particularly under a written guarantee or warranty, but the finance company can still be held liable, especially if the supplier or manufacturer has gone out of business.

PART EXCHANGE

You have the same rights as any buyer paying with cash if the deal includes an element of trade-in, for example in electrical stores offering part-exchange for old cookers and refrigerators.

AUCTION SALES

This type of sale has re-gained popularity and even houses are now being sold in this time-honoured manner. Once a bid has been accepted by the auctioneer and his hammer falls, the contract of sale is formed. The owner of the item exposed for sale is then legally obliged to pass it to the successful bidder who is obliged to pay the price to the auctioneer.

A potential buyer should always take every opportunity to have a close inspection of the property or item in which he is interested, **before** the auction takes place. This is because the conditions of sale usually expressly exclude liability for terms usually implied by law and to other sales although they cannot unreasonably exclude liability for misdescription. This is so even if the misdescription is made by the auctioneer in describing the item during the sale itself. If goods are misdescribed you should act promptly to reject them and claim back the price. The auctioneer is responsible for misdescriptions even if the true owner of the goods was not at fault in any way. It is, however, legal for auction terms to exclude most other warranties usually found in a contract of sale. This is particularly vital to grasp in connection with the purchase of houses or land by auction. In a normal house purchase transaction you would submit an offer containing many conditions which seek to ensure that the property is as you expect it to be and that there are no hidden defects. At an auction you are not able to impose any conditions whatsoever on the terms of the purchase and most auction sales of land will expressly provide that it is for the buyer to have satisfied themselves as to the amount of land for sale, title conditions, planning permissions, etc. Once the hammer falls, you will own the land, warts and all.

SERVICES

We enter into contracts for services when we go to the hairdresser's or leave our car at the garage to be repaired. The law implies terms into these contracts in precisely the same way as with the sale of goods. The service provider must use the usual care and skill expected in providing the service. If the price for the service has not been agreed then the customer is under a duty to pay no more than the going rate. It is always sensible to try to fix a price in advance but this is not always possible. What is a reasonable charge depends on the circumstances and Scots lawyers describe this as being payment *quantum meruit* (see Glossary, p. 263). If you consider that the service you received was not satisfactory and you have paid by credit card then you can demand that your credit card company suspend any payment. If the work is done so poorly that you consider you have received no benefit from it at all then you can refuse to pay anything or you can offer to pay what you think is fair for any part of the service that was adequate.

You must get the service you ordered within a reasonable time. The law would expect a simple or routine job to take less time than something highly specialised or complicated and therefore it is always best to try to agree a date or time frame for the work in advance. If the failure to provide the services in proper time causes you loss beyond the price of the work, for example you have had to call in another firm who tell you that the cost of the repairs has gone up because the situation has got worse, then you are entitled to seek compensation for the difference. You may also be entitled to compensation for hurt feelings and inconvenience, for example if your wedding photographer fails to turn up to take the photographs on the happy day.

EXCLUSIONS OF LIABILITY

You may be asked to sign a contract which seeks to put some form of restriction or limit on the service provider's liability to you. Examples of these are the signs seen in many premises, stating, typically, that the proprietors have no liability for loss of or damage to hats and coats, etc. Such clauses are valid if they are fair and reasonable in the circumstances. For example, you take your film of photographs of your child's christening to be developed and the shop has a sign saying that in the event of loss of your film it is liable for the cost of a replacement film only. It then cannot find your photographs. You would be entitled to argue that the exclusion clause is not reasonable and therefore should not apply. The position would be different if the shop offered two levels of service, one at the usual rate where the contractual limitation applied and one with higher charges where it accepted full responsibility for any loss caused by failing to produce the photographs. The law would then say that the exclusion clause was reasonable because you had a choice of which service to take.

Such a clause could also be attacked if the loss was caused by gross negligence. If your dress comes back from the cleaners with a tear, clearly caused by a knife being used to cut a protective wrapper, then an exclusion clause is unlikely to prevent you from seeking the cost of a replacement dress. It is important to note that any claim which exempts or limits liability for death or personal injury resulting from *negligence* in providing a service is totally illegal.

GOODS AND SERVICES

In some situations a contract will involve the provision of both goods and services, for example building a house or garage. In these situations the law implies certain requirements into the contract in very much the same way as in separate contracts for services and for goods. You should, however, be clear that the supply of defective materials may still lead to your having rights against the manufacturer. In the case of building a house the builder will be responsible for faulty workmanship and materials even if the person who contracted with him then sells the property on. It will make no difference whether the contractor does the work himself or employs someone else as a sub-contractor. The simple position is that you are dealing with your contractor and how he deals with the work is his responsibility.

Sub-contractors can create a difficulty if the main contractor goes out of business. You have no direct contract with the sub-contractor and, even though you may have paid for the whole job, if the defunct main contractor has not paid the sub-contractor then they will refuse to carry out any more work. The fact that they may have been on site and even have left work part-finished will make no difference. They have not been paid and unless you are prepared to make up the difference yourself then they cannot be expected to return to work.

You should therefore be particularly careful in paying for building or other similar work in advance.

PROFESSIONAL SERVICES

You can only have a legitimate complaint about professional services based on quality, not results. Doctors do not guarantee to cure your illness, nor do solicitors guarantee a successful outcome in a court case. The law was very clearly stated in a famous case on negligence and the test is therefore generally referred to as the '*Hunter v. Hanley* test' This states that professionals must act with the degree of care and skill reasonably to be expected from competent members of their profession. The most important aspect of this test is that it makes it impossible to establish that there has been negligence or breach of duty of care without the opinion of another professional in the field confirming that this is the case. You will find that if you wish to apply for legal aid to pursue a claim against, say, a doctor, the Legal Aid Board will insist that a medical expert's opinion be produced before your application can proceed.

In some situations negligent professionals can end up paying compensation not only to their own clients but to third parties who they should have realised might rely upon their opinion and could suffer loss. This is why many professions, particularly chartered surveyors, have clauses which prohibit the client from showing the professionals' report or opinion to anyone else without their express consent.

DANGEROUS PRODUCTS

Products may not only disappoint us but turn out to be positively dangerous. If an accident does occur and damage and injury result it is not only the person who purchased the product who may have a claim. Anyone who is hurt or whose property is damaged may seek compensation from the manufacturer or supplier. There are many ways in which a product could cause us harm but the most likely are:

- it is inherently dangerous, for example fireworks;
- it is used incorrectly, for example cleaning fluid which it is poisonous to drink;
- it is badly presented, for example unsafe containers or those with misleading or inadequate instructions.

People are still, of course, expected to use some common sense and would receive little sympathy if they cut their fingers on a razor-sharp kitchen knife. The usual common-law rules that relate to any accident where you seek compensation from the person you claim to be at fault apply here. These are the rules of foreseeability, causation, remoteness of damage and contributory negligence, etc. and are explained more fully in the chapter on accidents. A manufacturer will, however, be held liable for faulty components within his product, even if manufactured by someone else, or for faulty packaging, even though it is done outwith his premises. Where a product is safe only if it is correctly used then the manufacturer or supplier is responsible for ensuring that adequate instructions and warnings are clearly provided. Since 1988 the general limitations of having to prove negligence or breach of contract have been largely superseded by consumer protection legislation. This imposes no fault liability (see Accidents, p. 54).

FINANCIAL INSTITUTIONS

We rarely think that when we go into our bank and fill out standing orders or take out personal loans that we are entering into complicated contracts. The sad fact is that we are, but virtually no one, including lawyers, ever takes the time to read the banks' literature. When you open a bank account you agree to a contract with the bank that it will cash cheques written by you up to an agreed limit. An automatic teller machine cash card entitles you to draw cash up to an agreed limit. If we write a cheque which will take the balance of our account beyond the agreed limit then we have broken our contract and the bank has a number of remedies. The most likely is that it will dishonour (i.e. refuse to pay) your cheque and send it back to the person who sought to cash it. On the other hand it may apply a heavy interest rate to force you to reach an agreement with it to use your account in a manner to which it will agree. It will often seek to convert an uncontrolled overdraft into a loan, with fixed repayments over a number of years.

Stopping a cheque

You have the right to stop any cheque that you have issued, by simply instructing your bank not to pay. You can do this by phone but it is always preferable to confirm the instruction in writing. It was once the case that when a cheque was stopped the proceeds were still taken from your account and transferred to the manager's suspense account until the dispute on the cheque was resolved, but this is no longer the case. When accepting a cheque from someone else you must therefore ensure that you bank it promptly as you might find that the cheque is subsequently stopped, to your loss. Issuing a cheque with the sole intention of stopping it is fraud and could result in criminal charges but unless a particularly large sum of money were involved it is extremely unlikely that the police would take any action.

A cheque cannot be stopped if it is backed by a bank guarantee card and the cheque does not exceed the limit of the guarantee. You should always insist on obtaining a bank guarantee card number if you are accepting a cheque. Equally, if you are suspicious of someone from whom you are purchasing goods you must accept that you will not be able to stop your cheque, even if you discover that you are being swindled, if the amount of your cheque is below your guarantee limit and the seller persuaded you to give them the guarantee card number.

Crossed cheques

Crossing a cheque means writing on the face of it the words 'not negotiable, account payee only'. This is now commonly printed on most cheques issued by banks. A cheque is a bill of exchange, i.e. it is an order, addressed to someone who holds your money, to pay over some of that money to a third person. Bills of exchange have been used for centuries as a secure way of transferring the price of goods. Merchants from England were able to travel to Italy to purchase spices but instead of carrying gold, thereby attracting robbers, they would carry a piece of paper which enabled them to draw gold from a bank at the destination in Rome. To facilitate this type of trade it was made possible to pass on a bill of exchange to someone other than the first person in whose favour it was written out. For example, if the spice seller in Rome was leaving on a long journey himself and he did not wish to have the English merchant's gold in his house, he could buy goods for his journey and pay for them by signing over the English note to another Roman merchant, and so the process would go on. Eventually someone would want the gold itself and would present the note to the bank. There is, of course, the possibility of fraud or theft and therefore endorsing over bills of exchange has always had an element of risk. A crossed cheque is one which can only be cashed by the person whose name has been inserted on the cheque by the original account holder. The cheque cannot be passed on to any third party. It is therefore important to use crossed cheques to prevent fraud.

Lost or stolen cheques

If a cheque is lost or stolen the bank should be informed immediately so that the account holder is not held responsible for cheques written out by anyone else. If the bank negligently pays out on such a cheque it cannot charge the amount of the cheque to its customer's account. The bank also cannot debit the customer's account for altered or forged cheques. The customer must, of course, have taken adequate precautions for their own safety and the bank may not be at fault if the customer wrote the cheque in such a way as to make it easy for a crook, for example by leaving large spaces between words when writing out the amount. A bank must honour a cheque presented by a retailer who accepted it in the course of trade, even with a forged or defective signature, provided that it is supported by a cheque guarantee card and the amount of the cheque is within the guaranteed limit.

Cash cards and cheque guarantee cards

These cards should only be issued to customers who request them, or to replace or renew those previously issued. If you do not wish to have such cards you should simply send them back to the bank. Equally, if you do not want to use some of the functions of the card which are operated by a personal identification number (PIN) you can request that no such number is issued to you. We all write down our PINs but you should do your best to ensure that where you keep a note of the number is not likely to be obvious if the card should be stolen. Try to keep your note separate from the card. Banks are working hard to find technological ways to cut down fraud in this area. They have already introduced cards with the facility to include the holder's photograph and there are other forms of protection in development, such as cards bearing the holder's thumb print or even retina holograph, which are not just ideas derived from science fiction.

Bank errors

If the bank credits your account with money that does not belong to you then you will have to pay it back. You are under no responsibility to check your statement for any such overpayments and if the bank takes months to find out about the mistake then you can only be asked to repay the sum credited and not any interest. The bank will have to act reasonably on how it expects you to repay, particularly if in the circumstances you had no particular cause to be aware of the over-payment. In the event that the bank did not offer you fair repayment terms then you could complain to the Banking Ombudsman.

If, on the other hand, the bank dishonours a cheque or a standing order on your account when you are in funds, this could be of great embarrassment and inconvenience. You might also find that the person who expected to receive the payment from you has decided that you are a bad credit risk and added you to a credit register which may affect your ability to obtain credit in the future. Accordingly, a bank could be liable to pay substantial compensation to you for such an error.

Confidentiality

A bank is under a duty to keep confidential any information about your account. A bank should not disclose information about you or how your account is operated, even to other companies in the same banking group, except with your express consent. There are exceptional circumstances where a bank may be obliged by law to disclose details of your account to police in connection with certain offences such as major fraud, tax offences, drug trafficking or terrorist activities. The bank is under no obligation to tell you that such an investigation is under way.

INSURANCE COMPANIES

An insurance policy is a contract between the policy holder and the insurance company in terms of which, in return for a payment called the premium, the company undertakes to pay sums of money as compensation for the occurrence of specific events, for example death, fire, theft, etc. In some situations insurance is compulsory, for example third party cover for car owners. The contract of insurance is peculiar to that industry and has special conditions which do not occur in any other type of contract.

What you can insure

You can only take out valid insurance cover to protect against an eventuality where you stand to lose out financially, and this is what lawyers call **insurable interest**. You cannot insure property unless you are the person who stands to suffer loss if it is damaged or destroyed. The concept is particularly important in life insurance. You cannot insure the life of anyone in whom the law says you do not have an insurable interest. You can therefore insure your own life and that of your spouse. Businesses can insure key personnel because they can demonstrate the loss they would suffer if they lost the employees' services suddenly. You cannot, however, insure the lives of friends or even fiancé(e)s. This is largely to prevent you from seeking to profit from the insurance proceeds by inviting your loved one for a walk along the cliffs from which you do not intend that they should return.

Full disclosure

In general the law does not require people entering into contracts to volunteer any information, provided that they are not actually telling lies to persuade the other party to enter into the agreement, but insurance contracts are quite different. They are governed by a principle of law which states that persons entering into such contracts have an absolute duty to make full disclosure of all facts. Lawyers refer to this as a contract uberrimae fidei. This means that you not only have to give accurate and truthful answers to all questions on the proposal form but you must also volunteer any information which could be relevant. If you do not, the insurance company can treat the whole policy as void. You will find that most proposal forms ask you to sign an express statement that the contract is being made on the basis of the information contained within the form and that you have made all disclosures of any kind which might affect the decision to offer you insurance cover. The consequences of non-disclosure can be disastrous. The contract of insurance is treated as if it simply did not exist. You must also very careful about insurance contracts which are renewable annually. Each time the contract is renewed, the duty of disclosure arises again. If you do not disclose any changes in circumstances which have happened since the last renewal then, again, you may have a completely worthless policy.

Policy conditions

Insurance policies invariably contain terms which require the policyholder to do things or to refrain from doing things and if these conditions are not followed strictly the company may refuse to pay out on a claim. An obvious example would be a home contents policy which required you to install and use a properly functioning burglar alarm. If the company could prove that you had either failed to install an alarm at all or had one which was broken or perhaps just not switched on at the time of the burglary then it would refuse to pay out. You are also required to take reasonable precautions for the safety of yourself and any property that is insured. You may well find that if you have an extremely expensive camera normally only used for high-quality studio work but you take it on your annual family holiday and leave it unattended on your beach towel when you go for a swim, your insurance company will decline to pay you the cost of a new camera. It will argue that it was not reasonable to take such a valuable piece of equipment and leave it temptingly unprotected.

The level of insurance

This is another particular aspect of insurance policies. Generally speaking, it is the policyholder who decides how much insurance cover he requires for a particular situation or to replace a particular item. The underlying principle is that if you have an item that is actually worth £10,000 and you have covered it up to a value of only £5,000 then when you make a claim the insurance company will not pay out £5,000. It considers that you were only insuring half of the item and therefore it will only pay you £2,500, representing its half of the value of the item that you put on the proposal form. The justification for this is that the premium you have paid is based on the overall risk that the insurance company is taking: the more valuable the item, the greater the risk, and if you under-insure you are also paying lower premiums. You should always make sure that you obtain a written valuation of any valuable items that you wish to be insured and protected to the fullest extent. You should ensure that the insurance company accepts this valuation and if necessary you should pay a special premium to guarantee the cover you need. Insurance is there to protect us from the loss of items we cannot easily afford to replace ourselves, so being under-insured may be almost as bad as having no insurance at all. If you are in doubt you should ask the insurance company or your broker for advice on items of particular value to you.

Excluded risks

Policies generally contain a list of items or situations where the insurance cover will not be paid out, and these are known as **excepted perils**. Insurance companies will rarely cover damage caused by war or riot. You will also find that there are many other exclusions. You should read this section of your policy document very carefully to make sure that you have the cover that you expect and that you understand what the restrictions are. Common examples are home contents policies which often exclude cover if the property is left empty for more than 30 days. A clause of this nature would cause a difficulty if you decided to go on a world cruise and you suffered damage because of burst pipes while you were away. Different insurance companies have different excepted perils and it is worth shopping around or getting your broker to do so to find policies offering the terms that you wish, at the right premium.

No claims bonus

Insurers seek to limit their liability by trying to reduce the number of claims made and so they offer a form of discount called a 'no claims bonus'. If the amount of a possible claim is less than the loss of a no claims bonus then the insured will be discouraged from making a claim and will save the insurance company not only the compensation for the loss itself but all the attendant paperwork and administration. You must remember that it is a no claims bonus, not a no blame bonus. Once you make a claim, the insurance company is entitled to consider that to be an event which may affect your no claims bonus, even if you expect your insurers then to go on and try to recover your loss from a negligent third party. This is something you must consider if you are making a choice between claiming on your own insurance cover for a loss or seeking advice on pursuing recovery of the loss through the law.

Disputes with insurers

If you have a dispute with your insurers you can obviously complain within the company's management structure but if it is clear that you will receive no satisfaction from the insurers themselves you should ask if they are members of the Insurance Ombudsman Scheme. Not all insurance companies are participants in the scheme but certainly it covers the major household names. The Ombudsman has a power to award compensation but using the scheme does not prevent you from taking legal action against the company. There is also another voluntary scheme which some insurance companies support, called the Personal Insurance Arbitration Scheme (PIAS), run by the Chartered Institute of Arbitrators.

2 Accidents

Accidents can bring loss and distress into anyone's life and in almost every conceivable way. The home, workplace, public streets and even where we go for our entertainment are just as dangerous as ski slopes or race tracks. If you hurt yourself through your own carelessness then there will be no one else to blame but in this chapter we will look at what happens if the accident was someone else's fault or where the law imposes liability on someone because of who they are, for example your employer.

In order to claim compensation for your injury there are a number of legal hurdles to be overcome and in Scotland this area is called the law of **delict** (in England, the law of tort). The general rules are that:

- the damage must have been caused by someone who had a duty to take reasonable care not to cause you injury;
- the circumstances must be such that a reasonable person would have been aware that there was a risk of causing you injury;
- a reasonable person could have taken precautions to avoid the risk of injury;
- the loss you are claiming is for something a reasonable person

would anticipate could arise in relation to the kind of injury inflicted.

- you have brought your claim in time.

TIME LIMITS

Time is the enemy of us all but in injury cases the rules which exclude **late** claims can have devastating effect and you may lose the right to claim compensation entirely.

If you are going to make a claim on your own insurance policy for any loss you must intimate the claim to the company *as soon as possible* and usually complete a formal claim form within 14 days. Always check your policy details or ask your broker for advice on the time limit for claims.

You MUST bring any **court** action to recover your losses within strict time limits which are:

- **Three years** of the date of the accident for physical injury; or
- Five years from that date for other losses, for example damage to property.

This area of the law is complicated and legal advice will be essential but the rules do have exceptions which may come to the aid of a late claimant. These exceptions are as follows:

- injury to a child: the three years only starts to run when the child reaches 16 years.
- death of the injured party: if death occurs within three years of the accident then a further period of three years is allowed from the date of death;
- mental incapacity: any period of time when the injured party is mentally unfit will be ignored

- lack of knowledge: the injured party must know:
  - the injuries in question were serious enough to justify raising an action for recovery of loss;
  - the injuries were attributable to an act or omission of some one;
  - the identity of the person (or their employer etc) who com mited the act or omission.

  Beware – this exception will only protect you up to the date when the court believes that you could with reasonable diligence have been aware of the facts. You are expected to take some positive action to secure your own rights: for example, in one case the court held that the time limit ran from the time an injured party had a conversation with a police officer in hospital at a time when he was well enough to obtain details to make a claim but did not bother to ask. On the other hand, a patient who was told he did not have a disease connected to working with asbestos was allowed to bring a claim late when he was later informed by other doctors that he did indeed have asbestosis.

- latent defects: the time limit runs from when the defect emerges and causes loss or from the time when with reasonable diligence it could have been discovered. For example, when a solicitor allegedly placed the title to an hotel in the wrong name, the claim was held to run from the date the true owners discovered the hotel was being sold without their consent to pay off the other party's debts, because as laymen they had no reason to check title deeds before that although they could have done so at anytime.

- Section 19A discretion: the courts have the power to extend the time for claims (for physical injury only) where it is fair and equitable to do so under the provisions of this section of the Prescription and Limitation (Scotland) Act 1973 (as amended). This is a wide power but the court uses it sparingly and a very good excuse needs to be advanced: for example, in one case not only had the person who caused the injury died but so had the first person responsible for his affairs and then the person who had taken over, resulting in a chain of confusion and misinformation. The court held that it was not the claimant's fault that he ran out of time trying to unravel who to sue and allowed the case to proceed.

There are long stop rules which bring certain claims to an end (even if any of the exceptions apply), otherwise some obligations to pay compensation might go on forever. Liability for non-physical injury will cease after twenty years and product liability claims after ten years (see Product Liability, p. 54)

PRACTICAL STEPS

There are a number of practical things you should do immediately after an accident which may help you with your claim later. You may, of course, be too badly injured or otherwise unable to do anything but if possible you should:

- get the full names and addresses of all witnesses;
- call the police, if appropriate, and **always** do so if there are physical injuries caused in a traffic accident;
- insist that the accident is recorded in the accident book if it occurs in a shop or other business premises;
- take note of all surrounding physical details, for example place, time, weather, etc.;

- come back as soon as possible and take photographs of where it all happened;
- have photographs taken (professionally, if possible) of any physical injuries;
- preserve all damaged clothing, personal items and the like and look for receipts or other evidence of their value. Do not wait until months later when asked for these details by your solicitor or claims adjuster;
- get a note of any insurance company the other party says is providing cover for the accident and contact it as soon as possible.

DUTY OF CARE

We are not our brothers' keepers and the law does not regard anyone as having an absolute duty to protect the rest of the world from harm. The damage must result from negligence which was foreseeable and by a person who owed you a duty to take care. They must have failed to take the precautions that any reasonable person would have taken to avoid harm, and the damage caused must actually result from the failure to take that reasonable care.

Foreseeability

Reasonable people are assumed by the law not to want to cause harm and so the law protects them from claims if they cause injury by something that they did but which they could not have been expected to foresee would cause harm. Lawyers try to explain this with an illustration:

- a pot of liquid boils;
- the pot has a loose cover;

- boiling liquid pours on to the floor;
- a chemical reaction with new floor polish causes an explosion.

The reasonable man can see that there has been negligence in allowing the liquid to boil over and in providing an ill-fitting cover for the pot. The question is whether he could foresee that an explosion would result from the chemical reaction. This can be a very subtle test and foreseeability is a minefield, even for specialist lawyers. In the example, let us assume that the explosion blew out all the windows in the room; the argument would be that this was not foreseeable because no one would anticipate boiling liquid destroying windows many feet away. However, if the blast burned someone standing in the room then it would be argued that it was foreseeable as boiling liquid readily causes burns and the explosion simply spread the liquid over a larger area.

Scope of duty of care

The law has gradually extended this concept to place duties on as broad a basis as possible. The general policy of the law is to try to see that persons who are injured do receive compensation. A motorist, for example, owes a clear duty of care to other road users to drive in a safe manner but he does not owe a duty to by-standers who come along later to see the carnage of a road accident and are then thrown into nervous shock by the terrible injuries at the scene. There is no relationship between the negligent driver and the bystanders. However, if a professional person gives a negligent opinion he may be liable not only to his immediate client but to any third parties who rely upon his judgement if it was reasonable to assume that they might do so. This is why many professions impose contractual conditions prohibiting the client from passing on opinions to third parties without permission.

A duty of care can also be assumed by the actions of the negligent party. There is, for example, no duty in law for an ordinary member of the public to go to the rescue of a drowning man. However, if someone embarks upon a rescue operation they then assume a duty of care which could make them liable for negligent acts, for example hitting the victim by failing to keep a proper lookout on the rescue boat.

Probability of risk

The law does not expect every act we perform to be free from any risk to others. The likelihood of harm must be probable and the precautions taken realistic with regard to the nature and extent of the risk. A woman struck by a cricket ball which had travelled over a 17-foot-high fence some 80 yards away from the batsman (a stroke which had been achieved only six times in the preceding 30 years) failed in her claim. Closing down an entire factory after rainwater flooding has been held by the courts to be unrealistic although there was obviously some risk of accident.

The cause of the harm

The negligent act must have been the actual or predominant cause of the harm. In one case a child suffering from meningitis was negligently prescribed a massive overdose of penicillin. The child was thrown into convulsions but prompt medical attention saved the day. However the child was later discovered to have become deaf. An action for compensation against the hospital failed because there was no evidence to link the overdose of penicillin to deafness which was, however, known to be a common side-effect of meningitis.

Novus actus interveniens

This Latin phrase describes a specific problem where some new act, often by a third party, has intervened directly between the negligent act and the injury. The court must decide whether this new act broke the chain of events. This is not an easy task and each set of circumstances must be analysed step by step. For example, A is being taken to hospital with a broken leg caused by the negligence of B but during the journey in the ambulance a paramedic drops an oxygen cylinder on to the damaged leg and as a result it later has to be amputated. The broad approach is to ask whether the loss still generally flowed from the original act of negligence. In the example B **would** remain liable to compensate A, who would not have been in the ambulance but for the leg injury: what the paramedic did simply made the general injury worse. Amputation was therefore a foreseeable consequence of the leg injury, despite the fact that the paramedic's action obviously did not help.

Remoteness

The nature of the loss must be such that a reasonable person would have anticipated that the injury could cause such damage. Lawyers say that the damage must not be too 'remote'. This is a very complex area of the law and is difficult to describe in brief and simple terms. The most common problems arise in the areas of nervous shock and pure economic loss. Lawyers use the term 'economic loss' where there has been no actual damage or physical injury to a person or property but a cash loss has resulted nevertheless. An example would be negligently severing the electricity cable leading to a factory which loses a day's production. No one suffers any injury but thousands of pounds in lost profit might still be the result. In nervous shock cases the courts have tended to define the issue of remoteness by looking to any relationship between the parties. Close workmates, for example, might have a claim for nervous shock if they saw one of their team being killed by a faulty machine. A complete stranger visiting the factory that day might find that the court considered their claim for viewing the same accident to be too remote.

Defences

Aside from the obvious defence, that there was no negligence, there are other issues which can be raised, even where the facts of the claim are admitted. The most commonly met of these are:

- contributory negligence;
- voluntary assumption of risk;
- unavoidable accident;
- emergency action;
- immunity or lawful act.

Contributory negligence

The Law Reform (Contributory Negligence) Act 1945 states that the court may reduce the damages payable to a claimant by such proportion as has been assessed to be his or her own share of the blame.

This often arises in road accidents where each side criticises the driving of the other, or in work-related claims, for example that an employee failed to use safety equipment provided.

Voluntary assumption of risk

Lawyers refer to this concept by the Latin phrase *volenti non fit injuria*. This means that the injured person freely and voluntarily assumed the risk of the harm he actually suffered. This often arises in sports injury cases or claims by persons involved in hazardous employment. There must be clear evidence that the harm was within the scope of the accepted risk. For example, a football player cannot be held liable for causing injury to an opponent by accidentally tripping him or bumping into him but would be liable for, say, breaking the opponent's leg if he used a **deliberately** foul tackle on him. This act is outwith the rules of the game and was therefore not a risk that the opponent assumed voluntarily. Someone who accepts a lift in a car from a driver they know to be drunk will be told that they have no claim against him when he causes the inevitable crash.

Unavoidable accident

This is an event which could not be foreseen or guarded against. For example, a driver stung in the eye by a wasp and blinded is not responsible for losing control of his car.

Emergency

This is also sometimes known as 'the agony rule'. Actions in response to a real emergency situation will not be considered negligent. For example, a farm gate swings open over a track and to avoid hitting it a driver swerves but in doing so hits an oncoming car. The driver had the choice of hitting the gate or swerving and in taking a decision on which course of action to follow he might have been wrong but he was not negligent.

Immunity

The law makes some people immune from claims, usually on the theory that it is in the public interest that such people are able to go about their daily duties without fear of liability. The Queen is personally immune from any court action, as are foreign ambassadors and other diplomats. Judges cannot be sued for what they say on the bench, no matter how defamatory. Trade unions have limited immunity from being sued for damage done in furtherance of a legitimate trade dispute which they have instigated.

Proof of fault

The general rule

The burden of proving the facts generally rests on the claimant and if he fails to do this 'on the balance of probabilities' then his claim fails. The 'balance of probabilities' test is different to the one applied in criminal law (which requires proof 'beyond reasonable doubt') and simply means that it must be more likely than not that the accident occurred in the way the claimant has described.

Special cases

Parliament has from time to time decided that it is desirable for some accidents to be removed from application of the general rules and dealt with in a special way. These schemes generally relate to either where the accident took place, who the alleged wrongdoer is or what caused the accident. The most common examples are:

- the duties imposed on the occupiers of premises under the Occupiers' Liability (Scotland) Act 1960;
- work safety rules under the Factories Acts and associated regulations;
- liability for defective products under the Consumer Protection Act 1987 and associated regulations.

There is also special provision, in terms of the Animals (Scotland) Act 1987, for accidents caused by animals.

OCCUPIERS' LIABILITY

The policy of the Occupiers' Liability (Scotland) Act 1960 was to make it clear that the occupier of land or premises owed a duty to take reasonable care for the safety of people who entered them. The crucial questions are obviously 'What is meant by "premises"?' and 'Who is "the occupier"?'. The 1960 Act did not set out to define 'premises' and so each case must be viewed on its own facts. It is therefore a matter of interpretation whether fixed machines that transport people, such as chairlifts on ski slopes, are premises or not.

However, in common-sense terms, 'premises' covers most places which you would expect, for example all buildings, building sites, airport terminals, shops and offices, and also ships and aircraft, etc. 'Occupier' is defined as 'a person occupying or having control of land or other premises'. This will generally be the owner of the premises but need not be. You may own a building plot but if you have contractors building a house for you there then they will be the occupiers of the site until they hand over the keys of the house to let you move in.

The occupier is obliged to take reasonable care, in all the circumstances, to see that a person will not suffer injury or damage by the state of the premises or anything which the occupier has done or left undone. This does not mean that all you have to prove is that you had an accident on someone's premises and it then falls to them to prove that they were not at fault. The claimant must still show that it was the condition of the premises or the failure to do something or the omission of something that caused the loss. So, for example, if someone has filled a fire bucket on their premises with cleaning fluid instead of water they will be liable if you throw the contents to fight a fire and are subsequently burned but may not be if you drink from the bucket and are poisoned. A quarry near a busy picnic site may require to be fenced to be safe, whereas warning signs may be quite adequate if the quarry is in the middle of nowhere.

LANDLORDS

The Act places special duties on landlords. This is significant because the tenant would seem the obvious answer to the question 'Who occupies the premises?' but, due to the nature of leases, it may well be the landlord who is legally responsible for the condition of the property . The landlord will accordingly be liable as occupier instead of the tenant if:

- he is expressly liable for repair and maintenance of the premises under the contract of lease; or

- it is a domestic lease, for example of a house or a flat, and it is therefore an implied term that the landlord must maintain the premises in a tenantable and habitable condition (see Landlord and Tenant, p. 107).

There are also regulations which impose duties on landlords to have safety inspections on gas supplies and equipment.

WORK SAFETY

Employers have a general duty to take reasonable care to prevent injury to people or their property at the workplace. This, of course, can also be occupiers' liability if the accident occurs on premises. The duty to take reasonable care includes providing:

- safe working methods;
- safe premises;
- safe and suitable equipment;
- adequate training;
- competent co-workers and contractors.

In addition to these obligations there exist many specific regulations, some introduced by E.U. law, which compel employers to take precautions against specific risks. For ease of reference we shall call these 'safety regulations'.

Safe working methods

The employer must devise ways of performing tasks in order to minimise risk of injury to employees. This relates not only to how work is done, for example whether to use a shovel or a mechanical digger, but also to the conditions of the job. Employers can be held liable for psychological injury, for example depression caused by long hours or excessive workloads. Employers require to identify problems and take steps to improve conditions once they are aware, or should have been aware, that a problem or risk exists. Failure, or even just delay, in introducing new safety features, up-to-date machinery or reallocation of workloads can lead to a valid claim.

The most obvious risks come from activities such as heavy manual work or the use of machines with dangerous mechanisms. The employee does, however, have some obligation to use own common sense and to take adequate precautions for his or her own safety. If you choose to place too many boxes on a trolley to save yourself time you may be found partly or even wholly to blame if you then suffer an injury from pushing the trolley. If you ignore your employer's own safety rules, for example by not wearing safety equipment, you may find that you have no claim at all. However, if the employer was aware that employees regularly flouted the safety rules and did nothing to prevent this then liability can still arise even though the safety equipment was ignored.

Safe premises

This duty extends not only to the main workplace but to yards, accesses and any other place where the employee is sent to work by the employer. Slipping in an ungritted car park adjacent to the factory is the same as falling down an unguarded drain on the factory floor. All parts of the workplace must be safe and this includes floors, lighting, ventilation, hygiene and even general tidiness. Dangerous areas must be clearly identified with warning signs and any special safety equipment, for example breathing apparatus or protective suits, must be easily accessible. The general environment must be safe and comfortable, with adequate heating, ventilation, rest areas, etc.

Safe and suitable equipment

Equipment must be safe and appropriate for the job. Regular cleaning, maintenance and inspection of equipment is essential. Workers must also have adequate training in how machines operate, the proper purposes for which they are to be used and any safety or emergency features incorporated. This duty extends to non-mechanical equipment (including computers, where prolonged use can lead to eye strain and exposure to mild radiation). The equipment must also have safety features checked and updated where relevant.

Adequate training

The employer must provide adequate training not only in the job to be performed but in general aspects of health and safety. The training must be knowledgeable and relevant and if the employer cannot provide training at this level there is an obligation to hire in suitable professional assistance.

Competent co-workers and contractors

The employer must ensure that co-workers are properly trained in their tasks and understand their obligations to other employees' safety. An employer may not be liable for employees' isolated acts of horseplay but if a co-worker was known to have a taste for practical jokes and was not properly warned and disciplined the employer could be liable if he, say, welded a colleague's toolbox to a beam and the colleague dislocated his shoulder in trying to lift it.

The employer is also liable for independent contractors and other third parties they retain to carry out specific tasks in the workplace. If, for example, an employee were to be injured by the negligence of a contract maintenance engineer then his employer would have to pay the compensation.

Safety regulations

UK health and safety rules and recent E.U. regulations (commonly known as 'the six pack') impose even more strict duties on employers in certain cases. The form of liability is what lawyers call 'strict', which means that it is not necessary for the claimant to show negligence in order to succeed; all he need do is prove that the regulation has been broken. The Factories Act, for example, provides that all hoists shall be properly maintained, so that if you were injured by a hoist it would be for your employer to prove that the hoist was in proper and efficient working order and not for you to show what went wrong. Section 28(1) of the Factories Act provides that

> 'all floors, steps, stairs, passages and gangways shall be of sound construction and properly maintained and shall, so far as is reasonably practical, be kept free from any obstruction and from any substance likely to cause persons to slip'.

Strict liability can arise under other regulatory schemes and does not just apply to the workplace. There is strict liability for damage caused by nuclear installations and for certain breaches of the Environmental Protection Act 1990. There can also be strict liability for damage caused by animals (see p. 57). The general areas where strict liability for injury in the workplace is imposed includes:

- noise levels;
- environmental pollution;
- repetitive strain injuries;
- manual lifting of objects;
- safe machinery;
- safety equipment provision and use.

There are so many possible scenarios that it is impossible to list them.

If you are injured and think that strict liability may be imposed on someone, you should take qualified advice at an early stage. The environmental health department of the local authority can give advice, as will the Health and Safety Inspectorate for the area. They will be found in the local telephone directory. There is, however, still the qualification that the employer may have the defence of contributory negligence even where liability is strict (see Contributory negligence, p. 45).

PRODUCT LIABILITY

The Consumer Protection Act 1987 creates a scheme to protect consumers from injury resulting from defective products. The general policy of the Act is to place liability for injury and loss caused by such products on the person considered best qualified to ensure their quality and safety, i.e. the manufacturer. Compensation paid by producers means that those who profit are made to pay and consumers are relieved of the possible insurance bill they would incur if they had to protect themselves against such losses. The Act imposes strict liability where the safety of the product is

'not such as persons are entitled to expect'.

The legislation goes on to explain this rather sweeping phrase by providing that the defect must be considered in the context of:

- the manner in which and purposes for which the product has been marketed. This includes its packaging and any relevant warning labels or instructions for use;
- what might reasonably be expected would be done with the product;
- the date when a product was supplied.

Each case will be different but what the courts look to establish is that:

- the defect caused the accident;
- you complied with any warnings or instructions supplied; and

- you were using the product for a purpose that was reasonable.

We may, for example, find it incredible that a court in the U.S.A. found a microwave oven manufacturer liable to a woman whose poodle was killed when she attempted to dry it off inside a microwave. However, if we analyse this in terms of the U.K. legislation it is arguable that: the product did not say that the method of producing heat was harmful; other types of oven can be used for drying living creatures without necessarily killing them; at the time, microwaves were known to the manufacturer to use a form of radiation. After the poodle claim, microwave manufacturers were quick to plaster their products with warning labels and more detailed technical information.

The 'product' does not need to be produced by a manufacturing process and the definition of 'producer' includes suppliers of raw materials and agricultural processes. Someone who simply packages the goods is not the producer, but an importer of goods from outside the E.U. or someone who re-brands goods to say that they are theirs, for example supermarket own brand products, will be liable. The retailer of goods can also be liable if:

- the injured party asks the retailer to disclose the identity of the producer;
- the disclosure request was made within a reasonable time after the damage or loss occurs;
- it was not practicable for the claimant to identify the producer himself;
- the retailer fails to make disclosure.

The losses which can be recovered are limited to those arising from death, personal injury or damage to the claimant's property but do not include the product itself. This is because the loss of the product is a matter of contract or other consumer legislation.

The following defences are open to the producer:

- the product was made specifically to comply with the provisions of another U.K. or E.U. regulation;

- the product was not 'supplied', for example it was stolen;

- the supply was not in the course of business by someone who is of the producer class, for example at the 'bring and buy' stall at the local Brownie jumble sale;

- the defect did not exist at the relevant time, for example the product was modified or tampered with after being purchased;

- the state of scientific or technical knowledge at the time of supply did not give rise to an expectation that the defect should have been discovered. This defence recognises that technology develops and that what we thought was safe five years ago may now be known not to be;

- the defect arose through the incorporation of a product into another product, for example a component maker may not know the use the purchaser intends so he cannot be liable if his part or accessory fails because it is put under too much stress;

- contributory negligence by the injured party (see Contributory negligence, p. 45);

- time bar – a claim must be brought within **three years** from the date of the accident or the date when the claimant was reasonably aware or ought to have been aware that the particular defect caused the loss or damage. No matter what the Act provides, any action must be raised within 10 years of the accident.

LIABILITY FOR ANIMALS

The statutory provisions are to be found in the Animals (Scotland) Act 1987 but there are associated provisions in other legislation such as the Guard Dogs Act 1975. The 1987 Act provides strict liability for injury and this falls on the keeper of the animal. 'Keeper' is defined as:

- the owner or person in possession of the animal at the time;
- someone in charge of a child under 16, who is the owner or possessor of the animal at the time.

Someone who detains a stray animal in the course of their duty, for example a police officer, or has it solely to return the stray as soon as possible to its proper place is **not** the keeper.

The animal must belong to a species whose physical characteristics or habits are such that, unless controlled or restrained, it is likely to injure severely or kill persons or animals or cause material damage to property. The damage must also be directly referable to the physical characteristics or habits of the animal. So if you trip over someone's venomous snake or cycle into a stationary horse, the mere presence of those animals is not enough to create liability. It would, however, be quite different if the snake bit you or the horse lashed out with its hooves.

The Act also specifically provides that some animals have known characteristics. Thus:

- **dogs** and **dangerous wild animals** are presumed by the law to be likely to injure or kill by attacking, harrying, biting or savaging with claws or talons;
- **horses, cattle, sheep, goats, deer and other grazing animals** are presumed to be likely to damage land or crops.

The Act excludes liability for loss or damage caused by transmission of animal diseases. There is also an exception where the injury is caused to persons, animals or property present on land without authority or other lawful reason. Trespassers are, however, able to make a claim if they are injured by an animal kept as some form of guard or deterrent unless to have kept it there in those circumstances was reasonable. In the specific case of guard dogs there must also be compliance with the Guard Dogs Act 1975 which calls for proper training, competent supervision and other safety measures. The keeper has the defences of contributory negligence and voluntary assumption of risk by the injured party. The Act does not exclude ordinary liability for negligence and the owner or possessor of animals equally has a duty to take reasonable care that they do not cause foreseeable harm in the ordinary manner. The facts would require to be proved on the balance of probabilities and all the rules and provisions which we have already discussed in relation to ordinary negligence would apply.

WHO TO SUE

The usual answer is the person who caused the loss, damage or injury, but there can be exceptions to this where the law extends liability to someone else because of their relationship with the negligent party. Lawyers call this **vicarious liability** and the most common examples are:

- partners in a business, for the actions of their co-partners;
- principals, for the actions of their agents;
- employers, for the actions of their employees or contractors.

The theory is that vicarious liability stems from the implied authority which the person who caused the accident or loss had from the other person to do what they were doing. The partner was representing his firm when he gave the negligent opinion; the agent disclosed that he was acting for a principal; and the employee was on his employer's business at the time. It follows that vicarious liability cannot apply where the relationship is broken by action outwith the normal duties or scope of the relationship. Thus if a bus driver takes his bus on a run to the beach instead of back to the depot, the bus company is not liable for an accident he causes on the way. The original negligent party is not exempt from liability and can still be sued. This might be necessary if an employer went bankrupt but the negligent employee was known still to have assets.

WHO CAN SUE?

The injured party, provided that he is alive, is the only person who can raise an action for his loss or damage. The exception to this would be if he suffered from some mental incapacity or was otherwise unable to attend to his affairs properly, at which point the action would be dealt with by his curator or trustee (see Glossary, p. 263).

In the event of the claimant's death the action can still be pursued by his executors and the surviving spouse and dependants would have a claim for the loss they have suffered due to the death of their loved one. This would be for the loss of his company and guidance as well as for any actual financial support.

DAMAGES

Finally the court has found in your favour, but what do you get? Damages fall into two categories:

- **patrimonial or pecuniary loss:** which means your actual monetary loss, for example lost wages or the cost of repair to property. Wage loss is not only what you lost up to the date of the case or settlement but includes future loss if you will be unable to work again or your employment prospects are restricted;

- **solatium:** this is compensation for the general loss caused by pain, suffering, distress or inconvenience. Money cannot actually compensate for such matters, therefore the figure is not arithmetical but is very much what the judge thinks is fair in the circumstances. Lawyers will use previously reported court decisions to offer guidance on what might be realistic in each case.

You may also be entitled to interest on damages awarded but equally if you have received any DSS.benefits, the State may have a claim to recover some of its money and before any claim can be settled a certificate from the DSS compensation unit must be obtained which states how much, if anything, is due to them. Any sum due must be deducted from the compensation before it can be paid over to the claimant.

3 Rights at Work

The law has always provided a framework for the relationship between employer and employee but since the Second World War there has been such an expansion of the statutory codes governing the law of employment that it is now rare to rely on the common law in any question in this area.

However, it must said that any form of employment is capable of being interpreted by the court as an ordinary contract which can be broken, with the result that damages can be sought in compensation. This now generally called 'wrongful dismissal' and such claims can be brought in court or before an employment tribunal. This may be relevant if the employee does not qualify for the some of the statutory protections which we will discuss in this chapter. The damages will be limited to what they have lost and this may not amount to much. The average person is much more likely to seek to enforce their rights under the numerous Acts of Parliament and European regulations which now apply to the field of employment. The concept of part-time work really plays little part in modern employment law and unless expressly stated otherwise rights and obligations apply to all employees. The main provisions are:

- the Equal Pay Act 1970;
- the Race Relations Act 1976;
- the Sex Discrimination Act 1986;
- the Disability Discrimination Act 1995;
- the Employment Rights Act 1996;
- the National Minimum Wage Act 1998;
- the Public Interest Disclosure Act 1998
- the Working Time Regulations 1999;
- The Employment Relations Act 1999;
- The Maternity and Parental Leave Regulations 1999

The underlying principle of all of these provision is to remove general employee rights from the courts to employment tribunals (formerly known as industrial tribunals) and other government agencies such as the Equal Opportunities Commission. These tribunals were intended to settle disputes quickly and cheaply by using informal procedures. Employment tribunals are presided over by a qualified lawyer but there are two other members, drawn from industry and the labour movement. Regrettably, more than 50 per cent of the cases coming before employment tribunals concern allegations of unfair sacking and the backlogs in dealing with them have become quite severe. The legislation has also become complex and the allegedly simple procedures are often not well suited to the facts of a particular case. Full legal aid is not available for attendance at employment tribunal hearings but cover for verbal or written advice from a solicitor ('legal advice and assistance') is, and qualified advice should be taken on any employment matter at the earliest opportunity. The Citizens Advice Bureau also provides help in this area.

In order to have employment problems, however, you must first find a job, and many people now do this by approaching private employment agencies.

EMPLOYMENT AGENCIES

Until 1995, it was necessary for employment agencies to be licensed by the Department of Employment. This is no longer necessary but standards of conduct have been laid down and if valid complaints are made the Department of Employment can obtain an order to prohibit someone from running such an agency.

Employment agencies act on commission, which is payable by the employer only. A job applicant cannot be asked to pay an employment agency for finding work for them. To do otherwise is a criminal offence. The only exceptions to this rule are:

- in the fields of entertainment and modelling (where a fee can be charged, but not to the employer); or
- where work is sought overseas.

TERMS OF EMPLOYMENT

There is no legal requirement that the actual contract of employment be in writing but it is essential that the employer and employee clearly understand what the job entails and the terms and conditions attached to it. Employees are entitled by law to have their *conditions* of employment set down in a written statement, provided that they are employed for more than one month. The most important conditions must be contained in a single document so that the employee can clearly see and understand what they are being asked to do and what they are being paid. The conditions that must be covered are:

- the parties to the contract of employment;
- the date of commencement of work;
- continuity of service, i.e. whether employment with a previous employer is to count as part of the employee's service, and the date on which such continuous service started. This is important as it may have an impact on the qualifying period for unfair dismissal and any redundancy payments due;
- job description;
- place of work;
- pay, both rate and payment period, for example weekly or monthly;
- hours of work;
- holiday entitlement and pay;
- Disciplinary and grievance procedures (if more than 20 employees).

The employer may provide other details in a separate document, often called an employee's handbook. This may cover areas such as sick pay, pension rights, notice of termination, disciplinary procedures and other ancillary matters. There can also be references to a collective agreement with a trade union or even a statute for notice periods, sick pay, etc. but such documents must be made reasonably available to all employees. If an employee is not provided with a statement or is given one with inadequate detail they can make application to an employment tribunal to determine whether the employer should have provided the particulars.

EMPLOYERS' DUTIES

No matter what the contract of employment says, there are general duties that an employer owes to all employees. These are:

- to pay the employee for work done;
- fair treatment;
- health and safety (see Accidents, p. 52);
- equal treatment for men and women (see Equal pay, p. 71 and Sex discrimination, p. 73).

Implied duty to pay

An employer must pay an employee for work done. The amount must be specified in an itemised pay statement, which the employer is obliged to produce. There is no obligation on an employer to provide work for an employee as long as they are still being paid.

A written contract of employment may, however, make provision for lay-offs or short-time working. Lay-off can arise when an employee's pay depends on their being provided with work and the contract makes specific provision for pay to stop when there is no work. The question of whether a lay-off is only a temporary suspension of work, or is perhaps really a dismissal with the chance of being re-employed, is significant. If an employee is laid off for more than four consecutive weeks or for more than six weeks in total in any 13-week period then they can give notice of redundancy. This would enable the employee to claim statutory redundancy payments. Short-time working is where the usual number of working hours is reduced. 'Short-time working' is defined as work for which less than half a normal week's wages will be earned. Again, an employee can seek a redundancy payment if four consecutive weeks of short-time working have gone by or short-time working has been enforced for six weeks in total out of any 13-week period. The legislation provides for guarantee payments to be made to compensate employees in the event of short-time working. Guarantee payments must be made to employees who have at least one month's service. An employee laid off in this way is entitled to receive up to five working days' pay in any three-month period. The daily rate for guarantee payments is reviewed annually.

Insolvency

If an employer is forced to close down its business, all contracts of employment with its staff terminate. Employees will be entitled to wages owed to them and to redundancy pay. If liquidators carry on the business in order to try to save some of the assets, they become responsible for the employees' wages which then take first priority in the distribution of any funds gathered in.

Fair treatment

An employee is entitled to be treated by the employer fairly and with respect. The employer and employee are supposed to develop a relationship of mutual trust and confidence. Employers are not allowed to behave in an arbitrary or bullying manner towards employees and there are special rules that relate to sexual or racial discrimination.

An employer is not under a duty to provide references for

employees but the concepts of trust and respect imply that any reference which is issued will not maliciously seek to harm the employee's interests. The employer must therefore make sure that any personal dislike felt towards the employee does not spill over into a reasonable description of their working ability. The employer can be liable in damages even if the reference is inaccurate simply because of a negligent mistake. The employer owes the employee a duty of care to ensure that the reference contains only true and accurate statements.

EMPLOYEES' DUTIES

Employees have a general duty:

- to perform their employer's work properly;
- to conduct themselves appropriately;
- to promote their employer's interests;
- to keep their employer's business confidential; and
- to obey lawful and reasonable orders.

An employee is not under a duty to obey a plainly illegal order, such as driving an unroadworthy vehicle or falsifying safety records. It is much more difficult to define an unreasonable order. This a question of interpretation, particularly in relation to moving to a different place of work or carrying out different tasks. If an employee refuses to perform contractual duties that are properly their responsibility, the employer can withhold pay, provided that it gives notice that part-performance of the job would be unacceptable.

Confidentiality

All employees are under a general duty not to disclose information relating to their employers' affairs which they obtain in the course of their work. Whether a particular item of information comes within this general duty depends on the following factors:

- The nature of the job. It is obvious that some jobs, for example research chemist, are likely to involve processes and information which are of considerable value to the employer.

- Type of information. Not everything your employer does can be of equal importance and a distinction must be drawn between real trade secrets or other sensitive information and more mundane matters. The likely factors in determining whether a single element of information should be kept confidential would be:

  – Trade secrets – it is obvious that if you are aware that the work you do involves trade secrets or processes then they must be kept confidential.

  – Express condition – the employer may have indicated that certain elements of work are regarded as trade secrets and must be kept confidential.

  – Patents or inventions – the law states that an employee who develops any concept, process or device during the course of their normal duties must pass this over to their employer whose property it will be. The employee must also keep confidential the fact that such a patent or invention has been discovered. An employee may, however, be entitled to claim compensation for the benefit that the employer derives if the discovery is significant.

Wrongful use of information

When setting up a rival business or going to work for a competitor, an employee may not use any information which their employer regards as confidential. A former employer may ask the court for an interdict (in England, an injunction) to prevent such activity. The court must consider whether the employer has a strong enough case to justify interfering with the employee's freedom to work and must balance the relative interests of both parties. The court will consider the relative strengths of each side and the importance of the alleged breach of confidentiality. Employers often seek to protect themselves by inserting express conditions into their contracts, which restrict the rights of employees in connection with the use of information or future employment.

Restrictive agreements

These are express terms (usually called **restrictive covenants**, although this is very much an English term which has crept into Scots law) designed to protect the legitimate interests of employers from being undermined by ex-employees. An obvious example would be an employee leaving with a computer disk containing all the mailing contacts of the company. The courts will imply a restricted covenant into the contract of employment where it is reasonable to believe that the parties clearly understood that this would apply. This is really only an extension of the general implied term that the employee will not abuse his employer's confidence.

Restrictive covenants come in two distinct forms: those which restrict the ex-employee's right to make contact with clients and customers of the former employer, and those which restrict the type of work which the ex-employee may take on.

A restrictive covenant of the first type would probably state that the ex-employee must not, for a fixed period of time, seek to approach any customer or client of the former employer with a view to inducing them to transfer their business somewhere else.

The second form of covenant states that the ex-employee will not carry on a particular type of work activity for a period of time, usually within a certain geographic area.

The legal system must, however, attempt to balance both sides' interests and therefore the restrictive covenants will only be enforceable if they can be shown to be fair, reasonable and in the general public interest. These limitations are very important to understand, as the law does not allow an unreasonable restrictive covenant to be re-interpreted in a more reasonable manner. If a court holds that a condition is unreasonable then it is struck out. This means that the employer then has no protection and the employee and the ex-employee no restrictions. The general rules relate to two key factors: time and location.

TIME

The term of the restriction must be realistic, having regard to the nature of the work. How long a restriction should be will vary in the circumstances but anything between six months and two years is likely to be upheld. If a senior sales manager were to leave a local bakery factory it is quite possible that he could do a considerable amount of economic damage to the business in a few months and so he should be restrained from competing for perhaps a year. On the other hand, a sales assistant with a national company may have no real power to do the company any harm and a restriction of only a few months might be more appropriate.

LOCATION

The restriction must also operate only within a fixed geographic area. This might be as local as the town in which the business is situated, or the whole of the European Union. Again, the court would have to look at the type of business concerned and would also take into account for how long the restriction was to be applied. A senior executive of a garage chain with outlets in every major city in the U.K. might find the court feels that his employers' view, that he should not compete against them in the U.K. for one year, is a reasonable period. An estate agent whose company only sold houses in the west of Scotland would have little difficulty in persuading the court to throw out a restriction which prevented him working in England.

Public interest

It is considered to be in the general public interest that people are able to find work. The courts will therefore only protect an employer's restrictive covenant in so far as it can be shown to be necessary and specific in its purpose.

It should be noted that the issues of restriction on future employment are not matters which come before employment tribunals but are dealt with in the ordinary civil courts. An employer who believes that an employee is seeking to set up in competition or an employee who believes that his employer is about to take action against him should take qualified legal advice at the earliest possible opportunity.

Equal pay

The essential principle of the Equal Pay Act 1970 is that men and women should receive the same pay for work of the same value. This sounds extremely simple but in practice it is often very difficult to compare job titles and conditions unless male and female employees are simply doing the same work side by side.

Every contract of employment includes the right to equal pay, either in an express condition or implied by the terms of the 1970 Act. If the contract of employee A (who is female) contains conditions which are less favourable than those of employee B (who is male) then the law will simply read the terms as being modified by the Act, so that the conditions are equal. An employer can escape the rigour of the Act only if it can be shown that the pay difference is due to a justifiable reason other than gender. The employer will require to show that the difference is necessary to meet a real situation within the business and that the action is appropriate in all the circumstances. So if, for example, two applicants for the same job, of different sexes, were offered different salary conditions for the same post this would be a clear breach of the Act unless the employer could demonstrate its material reason. The burden of proof rests on the employer. Factors such as additional duties, extra responsibility, experience, length of service and where the job is to be performed can all be material factors. For example, if a university decided to attract qualified and experienced persons from private industry to head a new research and development department, it might be entitled to offer a higher salary to a man or woman from that background than it might offer to an academic applying from within the university. In that case it would be the qualification of having worked in private industry that justified the salary difference, not gender.

This aspect of employee rights is heavily affected by European law and there are directives which must be considered as well as the 1970 Act. More regulations are likely to be made, and anyone who feels that they may have an equal pay case should take suitably qualified advice at the earliest opportunity.

Sex discrimination

It is unlawful to discriminate in the workplace against men or women on the ground of their sex. The Equal Opportunities Commission provides assistance in such complaints and it is interesting to note that only 60 per cent of the cases that it handles are from women. European law also makes it unlawful to discriminate even if the employer is trying to achieve a better balance in its workforce (commonly called positive discrimination). This was once acceptable in Scots law but the Equal Treatment Directive (76/207) has outlawed this practice. Discrimination occurs when a man or a woman receives less favourable treatment than their female or male counterpart.

Direct discrimination might be moving a woman from what has become an all-male sales team, even if the employer did this because he believed that the employee might be uncomfortable in a 'macho' environment. Good intentions do not alter the fact that it is sex discrimination.

Indirect discrimination is where an employer imposes a condition which by its nature can less readily be complied with by one or other sex. Such a term would be challengeable if it could not be justified, irrespective of the sex of the person to whom it is applied, and it is to that person's disadvantage that they cannot comply. An example might be denying promotion to workers who did not do regular weekend working. It would be argued that women are more likely to have family commitments at that time and they could, perhaps, easily do the overtime hours by working a different pattern during the week.

Other discriminatory acts

The Act also states that there must be no discrimination in:

- the arrangements made for recruiting employees;
- the terms upon which employment is offered;
- refusing or deliberately admitting to offer employment because of a person's sex;
- the way in which access to training and skills development is offered;
- dismissing a person or subjecting them to detrimental treatment.

There is no discrimination if it is specified that it should be a man or woman who is employed in a job where sex is a **genuine occupational qualification**. This might arise where distinct physical characteristics are required (for example, a male or female actor) or where decency or privacy might otherwise be infringed (for example, the matron of a girls' boarding school). You are entitled to specify the sex of someone you wish to employ in your own home; for example, this means that you can insist on a female *au pair*.

MATERNITY AND PATERNITY RIGHTS

This is an extremely complicated area. It is essential that employers and employees take qualified advice immediately if a maternity/paternity issue arises in the course of employment. There are several basic rights and the regulations changed with effect from 15th December 1999 but most only apply where the expected week of childbirth was on or after 30th April 2000. The employee has the right:

- not to be dismissed on the ground of pregnancy or child-birth.This would automatically be regarded as unfair. An employee can be suspended (with pay) if the pregnancy made it impossible for the woman to do the job and there is simply no suitable alternative work that she could do. This might arise in a laboratory where exposure to radiation could be dangerous to the unborn child;

- to time off work for antenatal care;

- to maternity/paternity leave;

- to return to work after maternity/paternity leave;

- not to be subjected to unfair or detrimental treatment on the grounds of pregnancy, childbirth or maternity;

- to statutory maternity (not paternity) pay.

Time off should be paid at an appropriate hourly rate and there is no minimum qualifying period for employment before this right is acquired. The employee must, however, prove that she is taking the time off for antenatal care and the employer is entitled to insist on seeing a doctor's certificate or hospital appointment card after the initial appointment. An employer must not allow a woman to return to work within two weeks of having her child (now called 'compulsory leave') and risks a heavy fine if it does so.

Maternity leave

All women have the right to a basic 18-week maternity leave peri-od: this is now called 'ordinary maternity leave' This increases to 29 weeks after one year's continous employment: this is now called 'additional maternity leave'. The employee must give notice of her intention to be absent from work on maternity leave. Notice must be given at least 21 days before the planned absence. The notice must be in writing and state that it is the employee's intention to return to work. Giving such notice does not oblige a woman to return to work; it merely keeps her right to employment open.

It is no longer necessary for the employee to give notice of intention to return during the leave period unless she wishes to come back early in which case she must give the employers 21 days' notice. If she fails to do so the employer can postpone her return by 21 days. The employer may serve a notice within 21 days of the end of the 18-week ordinary leave period seeking confirmation of the birth and of the employee's intention to return. The employee must respond to this notice within 21 days or she loses the right to return but not her right of protection against victimisation or unfair dismissal/ redundancy.

Paternity Leave

An employee is entitled to at least 13 weeks' paternity leave after one year's continous employment for any child born or legally adopted after 15th December 1999. This is, at present, unpaid leave although there is pressure on the government to introduce some form of equivalent to statutory maternity pay (see p. 78). The employee must be treated in the same way as a woman on maternity leave and must not be discriminated against or treated unfairly in any way. Part-time workers are entitled to that proportion of leave which corresponds with the ratio of time worked against full time.

The Maternity and Parental Leave Regulations 1999 (No 3312) create a model scheme for parental leave which provides for notice by employees and a right to the employer to postpone leave for up to six months if justified by disruption to the business but Trade Unions may negotiate collective agreements for paternity leave which may improve upon but not materially alter the statutory scheme. This may be attractive to employers as such a negotiated private scheme may create greater stability within the workplace or be more responsive to the needs of particular industries.

Dependant Leave

The Employment Relations Act also introduced the entirely new concept of reasonable time off to care for dependants.

The act defines dependant as:

- a spouse;
- a child;
- a parent;
- another person who reasonably relies on the employee for care and assistance.

Time off must be allowed if the dependant:

- dies, falls sick, gives birth or is injured/ assaulted;
- is disrupted by a failure of the normal care arrangements in place;
- is a child at school where an incident occurs which must be dealt with by the employee.

Failure to allow time off in these circumstances can be reported to an employment tribunal within three months of the refusal and compensation can be awarded. Equally the employee must not be dismissed or suffer any detriment in the workplace for asking for the time off.

Redundancy during maternity or paternity leave

Where a redundancy situation emerges while an employee is on maternity/paternity leave she or he must be treated in exactly the same way as all other employees of the business. If there are other suitable jobs she or he must be offered the chance of taking one and the terms of any new employment must not be substantially less favourable. The alternative job offered must clearly be suitable and appropriate for her or his skills and experience. In the event that there is no alternative employment then the employee will be entitled to claim redundancy. The employer must guard against selecting an employee on maternity or paternity leave for redundancy on the basis of 'out of sight, out of mind'. The employee will be entitled to make a claim for unfair selection for redundancy if it can be shown that the fact that she or he was on leave was a material factor in deciding who should go.

Statutory maternity pay

This scheme is excessively complicated. Reference should be made to qualified advice or to the booklets and leaflets issued by the DSS. There is no equivalent 'paternity' pay although there is some pressure on government to make some kind of concession on this point.

RACIAL DISCRIMINATION

In terms of the Race Relations Act 1976 it is unlawful to discriminate against a person on grounds of colour, race, nationality or ethnic or national origins. The Commission for Racial Equality, which was established by that legislation, can assist employees who believe that their treatment at work has been detrimental to them as a result of this type of prejudice. The Commission issues a code of practice to assist employers in establishing procedures and in particular record-keeping facilities to monitor the ethnic balance of the workforce.

The term 'ethnic origins' covers more than the term 'race'. In law, a person's ethnic origins are determined by his ethnic group. An ethnic group is a distinct community with a long, shared history and identifiable cultural traditions including family and social customs. The most relied on features are likely to be:

- common geographical origins or common ancestry;
- common language and literature;
- common religion;
- being a minority group or being an oppressed group within a larger community.

An employer must not discriminate against a person in relation to the arrangements for interviews for jobs, the terms on which employment is offered or selection of candidates. The protection against discrimination continues after an employee has been en-gaged as there must not be discrimination in promotion prospects, selection for training or development skills and other benefits. Discrimination in selection for redundancy or dismissal will be unfair.

Direct discrimination

There is direct discrimination where one person treats another less favourably on grounds of race, colour, nationality or ethnic origin. This would include segregating workers by colour or origin even if this was for a worthy motive. An employer who moves an employee because it thinks they might be subject to racial taunts still discriminates. The law recognises that discrimination can be a subtle process and so if the facts of a case indicate discrimination and no other reasonable explanation is given then the court or tribunal may assume that discrimination occurred.

Indirect discrimination

There is indirect discrimination where:

- an employer applies a requirement or condition to a job; and

- the proportion of persons from one racial group who can comply with that condition is smaller than the proportion of persons from other racial groups; and

- the requirement or condition cannot be justified irrespective of the racial group or the person to whom it is applied; and

- it is to the person's detriment that they are unable to comply with the requirement or condition.

An employer may be able to justify a condition which would otherwise amount to indirect discrimination if it can prove that the condition was not imposed for such reasons. If an employer needs to call for Saturday overtime and that is the only day on which the work can be done, he may upset his Jewish employees but he does not discriminate. A company with legitimate hygiene rules which forbid the growing of beards would be preventing persons whose religion required men to grow them, for example Sikhs, from working for it, but it would not be discriminating against them.

It is equally discrimination to insist upon a particular ethnic or racial origin. A local race relations council that wished to appoint a Bangladeshi worker because of the high proportion of people from Pakistan in its area could not exclude suitably qualified Indians or Caucasians from the shortlist. It could do so, however, if the nature of the job was the provision of welfare services to a particular racial group. This is on the fairly obvious ground that it is really an essential condition of performing the caring role effectively that the service provider speaks the language and has a deep understanding of the relevant culture. A person from that culture is therefore the only suitable type of candidate.

Victimisation

An employee can make a complaint if they are treated less favourably because they have brought proceedings claiming discrimination or have given evidence or provided information in connection with any such proceedings, whether commenced by them or a co-worker. The only defence would be if the employer could show that the disciplinary action arose because the allegations had been untrue and were not made in good faith.

Proving discrimination

In addition to the areas we have discussed it is also unlawful to engage in the publication of discriminatory advertisements, to give instructions to others to discriminate or to put pressure upon another to discriminate. For example, if you are put in charge of health and safety at your factory and the directors tell you to make life difficult for black or Asian employees because they are supposedly too stupid to understand the new regulations, then you can refuse to implement such an order and any attempt to discipline you would be unlawful. It is, however, notoriously diffi-cult to prove that any specific act is motivated by discrimination. Employers often do not realise that they are operating discrimina-tory practices because the problem may well be subconscious.

The courts are well aware of the difficulties of proving racial dis-crimination at the workplace and therefore an employee will usu-ally be required only to establish facts which are consistent with having been treated less favourably on the ground of race. It is then up to the employer to furnish a convincing alternative rea-son and if it cannot do so then the tribunal could infer discrimi-nation. The employer can be ordered to provide information on the ethnic composition of the workforce in a racial discrimina-tion case, provided that it is not unreasonable to impose such an order. This will depend on the size of the company and the for-mat in which the information is held. If all the company records are computerised then an order is likely to be made but if it would be unreasonably expensive and time-consuming to assem-ble the data from manual records then matters might be different.

Exceptions

The law sets out to seek to eliminate discrimination in all its forms and in every walk of life but there are exceptions:

- employment in private households is not covered by the Race Relations Act;
- race can be a genuine occupational qualification for the job, for example a new member of a Polish dance group.

DISCRIMINATION AGAINST THE DISABLED

The Disability Discrimination Act 1995 sets out to try to enable disabled people to lead independent lives and be allowed equal opportunities in the job market. A person is defined by the Act as 'disabled' if they have a physical or mental impairment which has a substantial long-term effect on their ability to carry out normal day-to-day activities. 'Long-term' means that the impairment lasts for at least 12 months.

The impairment may affect the following:

- mobility;
- manual dexterity;
- physical co-ordination;
- speech, hearing or eyesight;
- memory or ability to concentrate, learn or understand;
- perception of the risk of physical danger;
- ability to lift or carry everyday objects;
- a medical condition which is in remission may still amount to a disability if the problem is likely to recur.

Duties of an employer

If a disabled person is placed at a substantial disadvantage in the workplace then an employer will have to take reasonable steps to improve conditions, such as:

- making physical adjustments to the premises;
- re-allocation of duties or working hours;
- acquisition or modification of specialised equipment;
- providing physical assistance.

The employer is only required to act reasonably and regard must be had to the cost, disruption and practicality of taking any particular step. An employer can refuse to offer a particular job to a disabled person if it can show that:

- the disabled person is unsuitable for that employment;
- the nature of their disability would significantly impede the work;
- training would be of little value;
- the presence of the disabled person would endanger the health and safety of other people.

The Act exempts small businesses with fewer than 20 employees. There is considerable pressure on the government to continue the programme of integrating the disabled into the workplace, and more regulations may be anticipated.

WORKING TIME

The Working Time Regulations 1999 implement European Union directions on the organisation of working time. An employee cannot be forced to work more than 48 hours in a week. An employee can choose to work longer hours but they must do so in a written agreement which must be kept in their personnel file. An agreement to work longer hours can be cancelled but the employee must give notice in writing.

The period of notice for dismissal, holiday arrangements and statutory minimum holiday periods will be fixed by law and holidays must be taken. Pay in lieu of holidays is generally outlawed.

MINIMUM WAGE

The National Minimum Wage Act 1998 introduced a legal minimum hourly rate that must be paid to everyone 18 years old or over and an increased rate on reaching the age of 21. The present rate for 18–21-year-olds is £3.00, rising to the full rate of £3.60 for those aged 21 or over. These figures are to be reviewed regularly.

STATUTORY SICK PAY

Employers are obliged to pay workers who are off work through illness and most businesses will operate their own scheme as the statutory regulations are very complex. There are exceptions to the rule: for example, employees who are over the State pension age when they fall ill. The best source of information are the leaflets issued by the DSS.

Another scheme exists called medical suspension pay but this only applies to workers who are exposed to hazardous substances in the course of employment such as ionising radiation, lead and certain chemicals.

TRADE UNION ACTIVITY

Employees who serve within the union movement have special rights. These are:

- paid leave to perform their duties or be trained to do so;
- protection from dismissal or detrimental treatment by reason of their union activities.

UNFAIR DISMISSAL AND VICTIMISATION

We mentioned at the outset that the common law of Scotland allows an employee to bring an action for damages if the contract of employment is broken. The statutory rights of employees in this area are now contained in the Employment Rights Act 1996 and the Employment Relations Act 1999. These provisions allow an employee to bring a claim for unfair dismissal or victimisation ('detrimental treatment', as it is now termed) to an employment tribunal. To bring such a claim, an employee must show that they have worked for the employer in question for a continuous period of at least 52 weeks. The calculation of this period includes accrued holidays and so it may still be possible to make a claim even if you have not physically worked for 52 weeks. On dismissal you should take qualified advice immediately to see whether you have a claim.

Claims must be brought within three months of dismissal and this time limit is generally enforced very strictly. Prompt action is accordingly essential.

Employees who are over retirement age for their line of work cannot claim unfair dismissal.

Note that the 'continuous service' rule does not apply to dismissals or other detrimental treatment claims based on sex or racial discrimination; maternity/paternity right ;trade union activities or membership; Health and Safety or other 'whistle-blowing' activities (see Whistle blowing, p. 88). Employees who have been dismissed or who have been the subject of other detrimental treatment in the course of their employment on any of these grounds may apply to an employment tribunal even if they have only been working a few days. The legislation also holds that dismissal for such reasons is automatically unfair.

The employee is entitled to a written statement of the reasons for dismissal within 14 days. An employer may seek to defend the claim against it but if it admits that the employee was dismissed then the burden of proof of establishing that it was done for a fair reason lies upon it. The reasons usually advanced by employers as being fair are:

- the misconduct of the employee; for example theft or assault;
- capability; for example poor performance or persistent ill health;
- illegality, for example dismissing a driver who had lost his licence;
- some other substantial reason, for example unacceptable absenteeism or failure to follow legitimate orders;
- redundancy.

Failure to implement a fair disciplinary procedure is equally a problem for employers who must show that in reaching the conclusion that the employee must be dismissed he or she was made aware of the problems or accusations and given a reasonable opportunity to answer them. Employment tribunals may order the re-instatement or re-engagement of an unfairly dismissed employee or order the employer to pay them substantial compensation.

CONSTRUCTIVE DISMISSAL

An employee does not need to hear the words 'you're sacked' in order to be regarded as dismissed. Employers who harass employees or create an unhappy environment in order to persuade staff to resign will find that the law is ready for them with the concept of **constructive dismissal**. If you have had a disagreement with a supervisor, where you were not at fault, but later your boss tells you that you have a bad attitude and your future does not look good, they will still answer to an employment tribunal even if you jump before you are pushed. Constructive dismissal can be difficult to prove and you should, if possible, take advice before you give up work if you intend to claim compensation. The new compensation provisions for victimisation for things like **whistle-blowing** may make these claims less common in the future.

WHISTLE BLOWING

The Public Interest Disclosure Act 1998 protects employees from victimisation or dismissal for making a disclosure of wrong-doings at work. The provisions came into force on 2nd July 1999. They are complicated and anyone who believes they are suffering detrimental treatment at work of any kind because of some form of disclosure should seek legal advice as soon as possible.

In general terms, for a disclosure which would otherwise be a breach of the employees' general duty of confidentiality to be protected, it must tend to show one of the following has, is or is likely to occur:

- a criminal offence;
- a failure to comply with a legal obligation;
- a miscarriage of justice;
- health and safety dangers;
- environmental hazards;
- the deliberate concealment of any of the above.

The Act requires that the disclosure must be made in good faith and to a 'qualifying person' such as the employer, legal adviser or a list of government officials and agencies set out in regulations . A disclosure to someone else – for example, a newspaper – will only be protected if it is made in good faith and not for the purpose of personal gain, where:

- the facts are substantially true;
- the employee fears victimisation by the employer;
- evidence is likely to be destroyed if the employers learns of the disclosure; *or*
- a previous disclosure of substantially the same kind has been made to the employers or qualifying person;
- it was reasonable in all the circumstances that the disclosure be made.

There are special exceptions where the disclosure is of an 'exceptionally serious failure'.

The employee who suffers because of whistle blowing may make a complaint to an employment tribunal within three months of the detrimental act (this period can be extended by the Tribunal if the employee can give a good reason why he could not meet the deadline). The tribunal can award compensation of such amount as it considers just and equitable in the circumstances.

REDUNDANCY

Employers can reduce their workforce because they genuinely do not need or cannot afford employees and, of course, they can simply go bust. The law calls this redundancy and there is a statutory scheme for claiming payment of compensation. The scheme is backed by the government so if your employer does not pay then the State must. All employees between the ages of 18 and retirement can claim. The amount is calculated by reference to the employee's wage (or a legal maximum figure) and the number of years worked. These figures are changed by the government from time to time. You should take qualified advice immediately if you find that you are to be made redundant.

Procedure

The employer must act fairly and consult with the workforce or any relevant trade union. If there are 10 or more employees, consultation must be at least 30 days prior to the proposed redundancies and this rises to 90 days for 100 or more employees. Consultation would include discussing alternatives to redundancy, for example calling for volunteers or re-deployment into other activities. Failure to consult gives the union the right to appeal to an employment tribunal.

Defences

The law presumes that dismissal is due to redundancy and so the employer must either show that the dismissal was for a legitimate reason, for example misconduct, or rely on the statutory defence that suitable alternative employment was offered and refused. Employees can refuse alternative employment if it involves a significant loss of pay and conditions or material changes in place or hours of work. An employee is not barred from refusing the alternative work just because they agree to give it a try. The employee may reject the job after a trial period of four weeks. The trial period may be longer if the employee's written contract contains such provision. Many large employers do use such clauses in the hope of avoiding discord amongst the workforce and to avoid claims.

4 Buying and Selling Houses

As a nation, we have always considered the ownership of land to be one of the soundest and most secure of investments; it is every young couple's dream to buy their first home. This is not so on the Continent, where renting is the most common way of acquiring somewhere to live and house purchase is generally for the affluent or an aspiration of later life, perhaps in the form of a holiday or retirement cottage. House purchase is often the first time that the man in the street comes into contact with the legal system yet this seemingly mundane activity brings with it a whole range of complex legal concepts: contract, family law, liability for negligence and what happens to our property when we die. The other chapters of this book are, therefore, relevant to the process we will now discuss but here we will focus on the practical sequence of events and what it all means when we buy or sell land or houses.

BUYING

The most obvious problem is supply and demand. An attractive property will generate interest and therefore competition to acquire it. You may have to look at several properties before you find something you like which is also in your price bracket. Advice from solicitors and estate agents is vital, to establish not only what you can afford but what you are likely to have to pay for your dream home. Few of us can afford to pay cash and so usually the first issue is where we can get a loan.

Loans

Property is a sound investment for a lender; it has not only your monthly repayments but the property itself as security. Loans of this type are, therefore, called secured loans, or 'mortgages' – from an old French word meaning 'dead hand'. (Note that 'mortgage' is not actually a term of Scots law; the correct legal term is 'standard security' but 'mortgage' is much more common in everyday use and is more readily understood by most people.) Until you pay off the debt, the house may appear to be yours but, as we will see later, you cannot sell it without the lender's agreement. The modern mortgage industry has so many packages on offer that it would be impossible and pointless to describe them here and you should shop around to find the best deal on offer at the time. There are, however, three main categories of loan.

Variable interest and capital repayment

In this method the lender calculates the total cost of the loan over the period for which it has agreed to lend, for example 25 years. It then fixes the initial monthly payments at the sum which will, if paid faithfully, mean that you owe it nothing at the end of the loan term. Interest rates, however, fluctuate with the state of the economy and if they go up so do your monthly payments but, equally, they can go down. This was the original basis of all loans. You can pay off the loan at any time, if you come into money, and all you will owe is the original loan plus interest less whatever you have paid back.

Fixed interest and capital repayment

This is, largely, the same as the type above but the lender agrees to fix (or sometimes cap, i.e. guarantee that the rate will not go up beyond an agreed figure) interest for a period of time. The fixed rate period can vary from, say, one to five years. These loans are attractive, particularly if interest rates look as if they are set to rise, because your monthly payment cannot go up, or at least not beyond any cap set, during the agreed period. There is a catch, however; these deals always carry a penalty if you repay the loan within the fixed rate period. The penalty payments can run to thousands of pounds and you must ensure that you take this into account when comparing packages on offer. Remember that you do not just pay off a loan because you have won the Lottery; the usual reason is that you have to sell to move, for example because of job relocation.

Interest only

The lender agrees to accept only the interest due each month, leaving the original loan (called the principal) outstanding. For example, if you borrow £20,000 then at the end of the loan term you still owe £20,000! This is because you have offered the lender proof that you have another way to pay off the principal when you need to. The interest rate will always be variable. The commonest methods are:

- life insurance and endowment policies;
- pension schemes;
- other property, for example office premises or holiday cottages, etc.

The danger here is that you always owe the lender the principal and you must be very sure that your other investments will realise sufficient cash to pay off the principal when called upon to do so. These loans were very popular, particularly endowment mortgages, but are now to be approached with a little more caution. Endowment mortgages dominated the market until quite recently because they were, for a time, tax-efficient. The government offered tax relief on endowment policy premiums to encourage saving and also relief on mortgage interest payments. This meant that by paying interest on the secured loan you obtained tax relief but not on any part that you paid towards the principal loan. The same money paid into an endowment policy to pay off the principal later attracted additional tax relief, thereby lowering the total payments. The Inland Revenue soon got wise to this and endowment premium relief was abolished some years ago! Do not take any loan of this nature without truly independent advice, i.e. from someone who is not being paid commission if they sell you a policy.

Pension-based loans can still be tax-efficient but you will need sound professional advice.

Surveys

Once you are sure that you can fund the purchase you must make sure that what you want to buy is in reasonable condition and find out what it is thought to be worth. All lenders will insist on a survey by a qualified chartered surveyor and even if you are lucky enough to be paying cash it is still prudent to obtain one. Surveys come in four main types:

Type 1

This is an assessment of the value of the property where the surveyor carries out only a visual inspection and does not guarantee that there are no hidden defects. The report will reveal any defects which were obvious to the surveyor. The price range for these inspections is from about £85 for a property worth, say, £30,000, rising to as much as £470 for a £500,000 luxury home.

Type 2

This is an assessment of the value together with a much more detailed physical examination of the building. The surveyor will do all he can to detect any faults in the building and will also say if he could not get access to areas where he thinks further investigation is merited, for example the attic. The price range here is £170 to £720 for the values as per Type 1.

Invasive

This means tearing the property apart and the fee would be negotiated privately. The surveyor may need the assistance of joiners to lift floorboards, etc. This could only be undertaken by special agreement with the seller but might be necessary if you were thinking of buying, say, a run-down stately home.

Specialist

Surveyors will often recommend that specialist companies, for example dry rot and woodworm experts, are called in to carry out a survey if the surveyor has found such problems or suspects that they may exist.

The offer

The dream house has been found, the funds are available and it has passed the survey, so now you must offer to buy it. Your solicitor will prepare a written offer and it is only this that has any legal significance. The seller may have told you that he likes what you have offered him verbally, but until the offer is put to him in writing these discussions mean nothing. The offer may be submitted purely on your instructions or because the seller has invited offers by fixing a closing date (see Selling, p. 103).

The offer is a lengthy and complex contract document which, sadly, these days does not just say who you are, what you want to buy, the price you will pay and when you can move in (these cardinal elements of any offer are known as Parties, Property, Price, Entry, or PPPE) but now must cover all kinds of related issues such as planning, alterations to the property, and the proper functioning of central heating and other household systems. The technical term for all of these additional matters is 'collateral contracts'. The offer will therefore stipulate that the seller undertakes that he is not only the legal owner of the property, will transfer it to you in accordance with Scots law and move out on the agreed day, but also such matters as:

- all loans secured on the property will be paid off;

- the property will be in the same condition as when you viewed it;

- any extras included, for example carpets or chandeliers, will be there on entry;

- planning permission and building control consent have been granted for the existing building, if quite new, or for any extensions to or alterations from the original design;

- replacement windows will comply with regulations;

- there are no local authority plans which affect the value or use of the property (e.g. a new road through the back garden);

- any appliances sold, including the central heating system, will be in good working order on entry;

- the titles do not have unusual or inequitable conditions, for example a right in favour of the local farmer to run cattle over the driveway or that you will be the only flat owner who pays for the roof repairs in a block;

- other modern problems, for example contaminated waste dumps nearby or old underground mine shafts below.

Offers are becoming more and more complex as solicitors try to anticipate problems which our modern lives throw up, for example divorce or bankruptcy, but in doing so they make it harder for the seller's solicitor to give a simple answer in reply. This leads to a longer lead-in time until the deal is actually legally binding and so, in solving some legal problems, another is created. The Scots system has always prided itself on preventing the notorious English evil of 'gazumping', i.e. the seller pulling out of negotiations because they have been offered a better price by a new player or are worried that their own house purchase may not go through. However, you must remember that until there is a concluded deal you can be 'gazumped' in Scotland as well. The longer the deal takes to tie up, the greater the risk.

Missives

The exchange of offer and acceptance is called 'adjusting missives' and the final deal is called 'the concluded bargain'. It is important to grasp not only the sequence of events but the legal concepts that underpin them. The offer is followed by a written acceptance but it is rare for this to be the end of the story, although for a lucky few it can be. The normal sequence is:

Qualified acceptance

It is vital to understand that this is really a counter-offer. The seller is in effect saying 'I will sell to you but only if you accept the following variations to your offer'. The qualified acceptance will list the conditions that are acceptable, for example the price, but will then make counter-proposals, for example that there are replacement windows but they must be accepted even though they do not quite meet the regulations.

Modified qualified acceptance

Again, really a counter-counter offer by the purchaser who is saying 'I can live with some of the things you have changed but either (a) not all of it or (b) I want something in return', for example a later date of entry.

The process goes on, with further formal letters going back and forward until the conditions of contract are agreed by both sides and the deal is then legally binding.

Conveyancing

The process of checking that what you are being offered is what the concluded bargain agrees, that all is legally in order and that you are getting a valid title to the property is called conveyancing. Solicitors who specialise in such work are called conveyancers. The transfer of title to land has been recorded by central government in Scotland since 1672 (in England, only since the 1920s) and we can, rightly, boast the most comprehensive land registration system in Europe. Until 1979, transfers were recorded in the Register of Sasines but there is now another system which created the Land Register of Scotland. The Land Registration (Scotland) Act 1979 introduced this new system to replace the Sasine Register entirely but it is being implemented area by area over a considerable number of years. For example, Glasgow now operates under Land Registration but Edinburgh is still under the Sasine system. The legal differences are too complex and subtle to discuss here at length but suffice it to say that the Sasine system records deeds but does not check that they are accurate, and guarantees nothing, whereas when land is registered under the 1979 scheme civil servants check everything and a land certificate is issued which the State guarantees is correct. This means that if, on a subsequent sale, say, the garden boundaries are found to be inaccurate, then the Land Register may have to pay compensation.

A Sasine purchase

The **purchaser's** solicitor will:

- Check the title deeds. This is to confirm that the buyer has a legal title to the property and to see if there are any restrictions or conditions attached to it.

The typical examination will be looking for:

– Rights of pre-emption: this means that someone else has first refusal on buying the property. This might happen when someone has sold off part of their garden to build another house and wished to have the protection of the condition for their own amenity. A right of pre-emption can only be used once and then it is no longer effective.

– Feudal burdens: these are conditions which have been inserted at some time in the past but continue to affect the property every time it is sold. They are, generally speaking, designed to protect the overall amenity of the property in the area, for example the prohibition of further building or of turning the premises into a public house. The Scottish Parliament has a Bill in debate which will abolish all of these conditions except where they protect real neighbour amenity rights.

– Common parts: there may be liability for matters such as access roads shared with neighbours but most commonly this is found in semi-detached, terraced or tenement build-ings with shared roofs, etc. The deeds must be checked to see if the cost of maintenance is shared fairly. The Scottish Parliament is also considering legislation which will abolish all of these conditions and impose one scheme throughout the whole country to share costs.

– Description: that the address and location of the property are accurate and the boundaries of gardens, etc. are stated correctly.

• Examine the search: the search is a written report from the Sasine Register of all previous transactions which have taken place in relation to the property, and gets longer as each new

sale is recorded. The search also records court orders which
might affect the sale, such as:

- Inhibitions: an inhibition is an order prohibiting the sale of
  or further borrowing on property to protect the interests of a
  claimant in a court action, for example for an unpaid debt.

-- Abbreviate of sequestration: this is the trustee of a bankrupt
  recording the fact that he now owns all the bankrupt's
  property.

-- Transfer on divorce: divorce courts can now order the
  transfer of property as part of a divorce settlement.

  If anything like this is found then some solution must be
  negotiated, for example the inhibition released by paying off
  the debt, or the transaction cannot proceed.

- Draft the transfer deed. This is called a disposition. It will be
  checked over by the seller's solicitor who will also expect the
  purchaser's solicitor to check over the documents he has
  drafted to release any secured loans, etc.

- Examine local authority certificates to confirm that the
  planning situation, road proposals, liability for drainage, etc. all
  conform to the contract terms.

- Prepare, on behalf of the lender, all the legal documents
  necessary to establish the purchaser's loan.

- Pay the price over in exchange for the disposition, signed by
  the seller, and the keys to the property.

- Record the disposition and mortgage deed at the Register of
  Sasines.

- Deliver the recorded deeds and the bundle of old titles to the
  lender who will store them until the purchaser's loan is paid off.

The work of the **seller's solicitor** is largely the mirror image of that of the purchaser except that he must pay off the seller's loan and record the deed which confirms this (the discharge). He must also account to his client for any surplus cash the sale has realised.

The seller may, of course, be buying another property and if so the seller's solicitor will have the headache of co-ordinating matters so that both transactions dovetail together.

A Land Register purchase

The process is very similar to a Sasine purchase but instead of the purchaser's solicitor having to examine a bundle of title deeds, the land certificate has everything collated into one deed. The searches take the form of reports on the Land Registers but their purpose is still the same, for example to check for inhibitions. The disposition (which is in a simplified form) and the mortgage deed must still go to the Register for recording but once this is done the documents themselves are physically redundant because the title certificate is simply updated with all the relevant details.

Collateral defects

Once the purchaser has moved in, in the standard Scottish contract there will be a clause allowing for defects in items such as the central heating system to be reported within a short agreed time limit, for example five days after entry, after which the seller is free from any liability. It is essential that the purchaser checks all appliances, central heating, etc. as soon as they move in, and reports any defect immediately.

SELLING

The owner wishing to sell has the same supply and demand problem as his counterpart, the purchaser. How does he attract enough interest to ensure that he gets a good price? Professional advice from solicitors and estate agents is usually the seller's first port of call and the price of these services is often a commission based on the sale price achieved. There is a lot of competition in the industry these days and you should shop around for the best deal, perhaps even a fixed fee. The legal process is very similar to that involved in buying but there are a number of specific issues worth considering.

Property misdescriptions

Selling anything leads to the temptation to gloss over defects or exaggerate the benefits of the product, and houses are no exception. The Property Misdescriptions Act 1991 makes it an offence knowingly to misrepresent the description of property for sale. This covers such matters as the area where the property is situated or its boundaries, etc. You must be careful to stick to the facts and be accurate in what is said on your behalf in sales brochures.

Closing dates

This is the practice of fixing a date by which all offers must be submitted. The traditional time is 12 noon. When the appointed time has passed, all the offers received will be examined and the best will be recommended to the client for acceptance.
Remember, in this context, that 'best' is not necessarily the same as 'highest' as the highest offer may depend on other factors, such

as the date of entry or conditions on collateral matters, which may not be acceptable to the seller.

The process of exchanging missives then takes place, as we have seen, to try to achieve a concluded bargain. There is one dilemma which sometimes must be addressed and that is a higher offer from someone else made after the acceptance of an earlier offer has gone out. This seller is legally entitled to break off the negotiations, if there is no concluded bargain, and accept the higher offer but the ethical rules of solicitors as laid down by the Law Society of Scotland demand that the solicitor concerned may no longer act for the seller. If you are the seller in such circumstances you will therefore need to change lawyers in order to conclude a bargain with the new player, unless the original purchaser has pulled out already for some other reason or simply agrees to withdraw without complaint.

Breach of contract

This can be a problem for a purchaser where, for example, the seller refuses to move out or perhaps there is an inhibition order preventing the sale but this is relatively uncommon and can usually be resolved more readily than the horror a seller may face if a purchaser does not come up with the price on the due date. The missives will have anticipated this situation and the seller usually has the following rights:

- to allow the purchaser a period of time to try to resolve his cash flow problem, provided that he pays interest on the price, usually at 4 or 5 per cent above the current base rate. The usual period is 14 days;

- to seek to re-sell the property and claim damages from the purchaser for any loss suffered. The losses will include interest on the unpaid price, the difference in price if no subsequent purchaser will offer as much as before, abortive legal fees, removal cancellation costs, etc. Sellers may often have to extend the period of grace before attempting to re-sell the property, on the practical ground that it may take some time to do so or if the purchase price was particularly attractive. Damages for breach of contract are all very well if the purchaser has assets from which to meet them but as it is usually a cash flow problem which has created the difficulty this is not often the case. A practical solution is generally preferable to rushing into court.

AUCTION SALES

Selling land and houses by auction has recently become popular, particularly to sell surplus properties held by organisations, for example water boards selling off cottages no longer needed by employees. They are also often used by lenders who have repossessed property from borrowers which they have been unable to sell by conventional methods. The lender has no desire to be a landlord and wishes to be rid of the property somehow. The important thing to remember is that the sale is legally concluded when the auctioneer's hammer falls. There is no process of adjusting missives. The auction sale particulars will set out all the conditions of sale and the purchaser is responsible for making his own enquiries about the property before the auction as this cannot be done afterwards. The seller is only interested in being paid the hammer price (less the auctioneer's commission) and the buyer takes the property tantum et tale, which is loosely translated from the Latin as 'warts and all'. This is definitely a case of 'buyer beware' but there can be bargains to be had for the well-prepared purchaser.

D.I.Y. TRANSACTIONS

The investment that we all make in our homes is, for most people, the largest single transaction they make in their lives. It is legally quite possible for you to carry out the whole process your-self, both buying and selling, but in these highly competitive times the fees being charged by solicitors and estate agents have fallen considerably over the years and the risk of getting it wrong is rarely acceptable when balanced against the fees likely to be charged. Indeed, in the standard modern transaction it is H.M. Government which makes the real profit. The government charges not only fairly hefty sums for recording deeds in both the Sasine and Land Registers but also stamp duty on all properties worth over £60,000. You will have to pay these disbursements, together with the cost of the searches and local authority property enquiry certificates, etc., whether you retain professional help or not.

5 Landlord and Tenant

We all need somewhere to live and the commonest alternative to purchase is to rent. Many of us will live in rented accommodation at some time in our lives and in this chapter we will look at :

- private sector tenancies; and
- public sector tenancies.

These forms of tenancy apply only to **residential property** and the law relating to commercial tenancies of business premises is different.

PRIVATE SECTOR TENANCIES

These are provided by private property owners, whether individuals, partnerships or limited companies.

Such tenancies are now governed largely by Part 2 of the Housing (Scotland) Act 1988 which created two types of tenancy: the **assured tenancy** and the **short assured tenancy**. Any tenancy agreement entered into before 2 January 1989 and which is still continuing is governed by the previous legislation. The intention behind the 1988 Act was to relax the level of regulation which until then had been imposed upon the landlord and which, it was believed, was discouraging the development of the private rented sector.

The tenancy agreement

The phrases 'tenancy agreement' or 'residential lease' simply mean the contract between the landlord and the tenant.

'**Contractual tenancy**' is an agreement to let negotiated between a landlord and tenant. This should be in writing (see below) but can be created if the tenant can prove what the law considers the four essential elements:

- parties, i.e. landlord(s) and tenant(s);
- subjects, i.e. the property to be let;
- rent;
- duration, i.e. the period of time for which the property is to be let.

The landlord has a duty to draw up the lease, setting out the terms of the tenancy which should include the details given above and all other matters relative to the agreement, such as the mechanism for rent increases, liability for repair and decoration, etc., and any restrictions or conditions regarding the use of the property (e.g. no pets). The lease must be signed by the landlord and the tenant and witnessed. The landlord must provide the tenant with a copy of the lease and must not charge for this. If the landlord refuses to provide a written tenancy agreement, the tenant can go to court to have one drawn up.

A '**statutory assured tenancy**' is the term used to describe the right of occupation given by the 1988 Act to a tenant whose contractual tenancy has come to an end (perhaps because it was for a fixed period) but he or she has not been legally required by the landlord to move out or given a new contractual tenancy.

The law on private sector tenancies is complex and, whether you are a landlord or a tenant, it is always advisable to seek professional advice on the creation and dissolution of residential leases.

Types of tenancy

As was mentioned above, the 1988 Act created two types of tenancy:

- the assured tenancy; and
- the short assured tenancy.

Assured tenancy

This is a letting of all or part of the house or flat as a separate dwelling where the tenant is an individual and occupies the house as their only or principal home.

HOUSE LET AS A SEPARATE DWELLING

This would include both part of a house and a flat. It also covers the situation where you rent a room in a flat (but not where there is a resident landlord) where you share parts of the accommodation (e.g. bathroom, kitchen and living room) with other tenants.

TENANT MUST BE AN INDIVIDUAL

A company or business partnership cannot be the tenant under an assured tenancy.

ONLY OR PRINCIPAL HOME

There is no definition of this. Periods of absence from a house do not by themselves preclude a house from being an only or principal home. The matter is one of fact. The tenant must have a real and substantial connection with the house in question rather than with any other house.

WHEN IS A LETTING NOT AN ASSURED TENANCY?

The following are not assured tenancies:

- a tenancy entered into before 2 January 1989;
- a tenancy of a house which is not the tenant's only or principal home;
- a tenancy with a rent of less than £6 per week or no rent at all;
- a tenancy of a house which forms part of a shop or premises licensed to sell alcohol for consumption on the premises;
- a tenancy of agricultural land and holdings;
- occupation of halls of residence or flats let by designated educational bodies to students;
- a letting for a holiday home;
- a letting by the Crown or a government department;
- public sector tenancies, i.e. those provided by local authorities or certain housing associations;

- letting where there is a resident landlord, i.e. where the landlord lives in the same house or flat as the tenant. There must be direct access between the landlord's part of the house and the tenant's part if the landlord is to be regarded as resident;
- a tenancy under a shared ownership agreement;
- occupation of temporary accommodation for homeless persons provided by a local authority.

SECURITY OF TENURE

An assured tenancy gives the tenant **security of tenure**. This means that even once the period of the tenancy under the tenancy agreement has ended the tenant has the right to continue living in the property unless the landlord is entitled to possession under one of the grounds discussed below. The landlord will require to obtain a court order to enforce his right of possession.

Short assured tenancy

This is a special type of assured tenancy. It must be for a **minimum** of **six months**. To create a short assured tenancy the landlord must, before the tenancy agreement is signed, serve a special notice on the tenant. This notice is called an AT5 and it explains to the tenant that the tenancy being offered is a short assured tenancy.

N.B. A tenant under a short assured tenancy has **no** security of tenure. The landlord is entitled to re-possess the house on the expiry of the tenancy agreement, provided that:

- they have served the AT5;
- they serve the proper notices to bring the tenancy to an end.

If the landlord does not serve the AT5 notice on the tenant then the tenancy agreement is an assured tenancy which gives the tenant security of tenure. A tenant under a short assured tenancy can apply to the Rent Assessment Committee for determination of a market rent for the property.

If, on the expiry of one short assured tenancy, the landlord offers the same tenant another short assured tenancy of the same property, he need not serve another AT5 and the tenancy can be for less than six months.

N.B. If you wish to rent out your own house (e.g. while you are working abroad) or a second property you have purchased as an investment, this should always be done under a short assured tenancy agreement to ensure that you have an absolute right to re-possess the property on expiry of the period of the tenancy agreement. If you allow the tenant to occupy under an assured tenancy you have no automatic right to re-possess on expiry of the tenancy period.

Rent

The rent for an assured or short assured tenancy is negotiated between the landlord and tenant on the basis of a **market rent**. A market rent is what a willing landlord would accept and a willing tenant would pay for that property in that area.

If the landlord and tenant agree, the rent can be varied at any time. Often tenancy agreements for a period of a year or more will have built-in mechanisms for rent increases. For example, this can be done by providing that the rent will increase by the rate of inflation each year or will increase by a set percentage each year.

Where the landlord and tenant cannot agree then there are three methods of seeking a rent adjustment:

- where a contractual tenancy has come to an end and a statutory assured tenancy has been created, either the landlord or the tenant may propose new tenancy terms and/or a rent adjustment. This is done by one party serving on the other a specific form known as an AT1;

- a landlord can propose a rent increase at any time during a statutory assured tenancy but not more than once a year. This is done by serving notice AT2 on the tenant;

- a tenant under a short assured tenancy can ask the Rent Assessment Committee to determine a market rent for the property. This is done by serving form AT4 on the landlord.

If the landlord and tenant cannot reach agreement under the first two grounds above, either can then apply to the Rent Assessment Committee for determination of the rent adjustment. The application must be made on specific forms and within specified time limits. The Committee will fix a market rent for the property. It can base its decision on written submissions from the landlord and tenant but they will usually ask both parties to attend a hearing at which they will be given an opportunity to put their cases.

Re-gaining possession of an assured tenancy

To bring a contractual (i.e. written) tenancy to an end a landlord must serve a **notice to quit** on the tenant.

Some tenancy agreements include a clause which says that the tenant is obliged to quit the property at the end of the contractual tenancy without the landlord having to serve a notice to quit or take any further action. **Such clauses are of no effect** and cannot be relied upon by the landlord. He **must** serve a notice to quit and obtain a possession order before he can evict the tenant.

The notice to quit must:

- be in writing;
- state the period of notice after which it will become effective;
- make it clear that even after the period of given notice has run out the tenant is entitled to remain in the property until the landlord gets a court order to evict him (known as an order for possession);
- explain that the notice to quit brings the contractual tenancy to an end and that this is immediately replaced by a statutory assured tenancy (see p. 109) and that the landlord will be entitled to propose new terms and/or a rent adjustment.

N.B. A landlord cannot change an assured tenancy to a short assured tenancy without the tenant's agreement.

If the notice to quit does not contain the above information it is invalid and does not bring the contractual tenancy to an end.

If a **tenant** wants to serve a notice to quit on his landlord it must be in writing and must give the landlord the period of notice provided in the lease. It does **not** need to provide the information given above.

Minimum period for notices to quit

Usually the lease specifies the period of the notice to quit. If it does not, then certain rules apply:

- if the lease is for less than four months, the period of notice is one third of the total length of the lease, subject to a minimum of 28 days;

- if the lease is for four months or more, the period of notice is 40 days.

The lease agreement can provide for longer periods than these but cannot shorten these periods.

What happens if no notice to quit is served?

The tenancy continues on the same terms and for the same period.

N.B. If you are a tenant who intends to move out at the end of your contractual tenancy, make sure you give notice to quit otherwise you could remain liable for the rent for the continuing tenancy even though you have moved out.

Notice of proceedings

As we have seen, a notice to quit brings the contractual tenancy to an end. If the tenant moves out voluntarily the landlord need do no more to re-gain possession. However, if the tenant exercises his right to remain in the property the landlord must get a court order for possession. Before he can raise court proceedings he must serve a notice of proceedings on the tenant. This notice (called an AT6) must:

- inform the tenant that the landlord is raising proceedings for re-possession;
- set out the ground(s) on which possession is sought.

PERIOD OF NOTICE FOR NOTICE OF PROCEEDINGS

Under Grounds 1, 2, 5, 6, 7, 9 or 17 (see below) the period is two months. Otherwise it is two weeks. The notice of proceedings can be served at the same time as, or after, the notice to quit.

Grounds for possession

The landlord can only get a court order for possession of a house under an assured tenancy on one or more of the 17 grounds specified in the Act. On Grounds 1–8 (which are generally known as the **mandatory grounds**) the court **must** grant the possession order if the ground is established.

On Grounds 9–17 (generally known as the **discretionary grounds**) the court must be satisfied:

- not only that the ground is established; but also
- that it is in all the circumstances **reasonable** to grant possession to the landlord.

The grounds are:

MANDATORY GROUNDS

Ground 1

The landlord needs the property for himself or his spouse for use as the principal home for one or both of them. The property must have been the landlord's only or principal home before the tenancy was granted. The landlord has to give the tenant notice in writing before the beginning of the tenancy that he might want to recover possession on this ground (unless the sheriff decides that it is reasonable to dispense with the requirement of notice).

Ground 2

The property is subject to a mortgage and the lender (i.e. the bank or building society) is entitled to sell the property because the landlord failed to keep to the conditions of the loan. The landlord must give the tenant notice in writing before the beginning of the tenancy that possession might be recovered on this ground (unless the sheriff decides that it is reasonable to dispense with the requirement of notice).

N.B. If you buy a property on a mortgage and then let it out, you may be in breach of the mortgage agreement. You must get permission from your bank or building society before you let out the property to others.

Ground 3

The property is usually used for holiday letting. A landlord can let such a property to a tenant, who does not want it for a holiday, for a fixed tenancy of no more than eight months, provided that the property was occupied for holiday letting during the preceding 12 months and the landlord gave the tenant notice in writing before the beginning of the tenancy that possession might be recovered on this ground.

Ground 4

The premises belong to an educational institution which normally lets them to students and which wants the premises back again for this purpose.

Ground 5

The house or room is normally held for the use of a minister or full-time lay missionary in connection with his work and is required again for this purpose. Again, the landlord has to give the tenant notice in writing before the beginning of the tenancy that possession might be recovered on this ground.

Ground 6

The landlord needs to have possession of the property in order to carry out demolition or reconstruction or substantial works on the property which can only be carried out if the tenant gives up possession. If possession is granted on this ground the landlord must pay the tenant's reasonable removing costs.

Ground 7

The tenancy has been inherited by a new tenant under the will or the rules of intestate succession (see Death, p. 248) of the original tenant. The landlord must raise proceedings within 12 months of the death of the original tenant, or of the date on which the landlord learned of his death. This ground does not apply to succession by spouses (see Death of tenant, p. 120).

Ground 8

At least three months' rent is in arrears **both** on the date when the notice of proceedings is served **and** at the date of the court hearing.

DISCRETIONARY GROUNDS

Ground 9

Suitable alternative accommodation is available or will be available for the tenant if the order for possession is granted.

If the landlord is granted possession on this ground he must pay the tenant's reasonable removing costs.

Ground 10

The tenant has given notice to quit which has expired but he has stayed on in the property. The landlord must raise these proceedings no later than six months after expiry of the notice to quit served by the tenant.

Ground 11

The tenant has persistently delayed in paying rent.

N.B. This ground still applies even if the tenant is not actually in arrears at the start of court proceedings.

Ground 12

Some rent is unpaid at the start of court proceedings and at the time of serving notice of proceedings (even if there has been no persistent delay in paying rent).

Ground 13

Any obligation of the tenancy (other than the obligation to pay rent) has been broken by the tenant.

Ground 14

The tenant has allowed or caused damage to the house or common parts of the building in which the house is situated.

Ground 15

The tenant or anyone living with him has caused a nuisance or annoyance to neighbours or has been convicted of immoral or illegal use of the premises.

Ground 16

The tenant has damaged the furniture or allowed it to become damaged.

Ground 17

The house was let to the tenant because he was employed by the landlord and the tenant is no longer employed by the landlord.

Re-gaining possession of a short assured tenancy

The landlord must still serve a notice to quit and notice of proceedings as above. Again, the tenant is entitled to stay on until the landlord obtains a possession order but the court **must** grant the order if it is established that the tenancy is a short assured tenancy and the notice to quit and notice of proceedings have been served.

A landlord under a short assured tenancy can also re-gain possession on any of the 17 grounds referred to above.

Death of tenant

If a husband, wife or cohabitee of the original tenant was living in the house immediately before the tenant died, he or she automatically gains the tenancy on that tenant's death. The original tenant must not have succeeded to the tenancy himself in this way. There is no provision for other family members, such as children, to succeed to an assured tenancy even if they are living with the original tenant at the time of his death, unless the tenancy agreement specifically provides for this.

Repairs and improvements

Who is responsible for repairs?

The landlord must keep the property wind- and watertight and in good tenantable condition. The landlord is also responsible for repair of the structure and exterior of the property. He must also keep in repair and proper working order:

- sinks, baths and toilets;
- any installations for supplying water, gas and electricity; and
- any installations for heating water (immersion heater, gas boiler) and heating space (e.g. fires and radiators).

There are also specific regulations requiring the landlord to have any gas installations checked annually for safety. A record must be kept of the **dates of inspections**, the **identity and qualifications** of the inspectors and any **remedial works** carried out. The tenant is entitled to a copy of the record. Failure to comply with the regulations is a *criminal offence* and the landlord could sued in the civil courts for damages. Where the property is let, furnished all furniture and furnishings must pass the 'cigarette test' and 'ignitability test' as defined in the Furniture and Furnishings (Fire) (Safety) Amendment Regulations 1988 (as amended in 1993).

Otherwise, responsibility for repairs depends upon the terms of the tenancy agreement itself.

Access for repairs

The tenant must give the landlord access to the property and all reasonable facilities to do any repairs the landlord is required or entitled to carry out.

Where the landlord is responsible in law for the repairs, they may enter the property to inspect its condition and state of repair, provided that the tenant is given 24 hours' notice in writing and the inspection is carried out at a reasonable time of day.

Protection from harassment and eviction

The law provides two forms of protection:

- criminal prosecution; and

- civil action for damages.

The offence of unlawful eviction or harassment is committed if a person unlawfully deprives the residential occupier of the premises.

The 'residential occupier' is a contractual or statutorily protected tenant, a lodger, a service occupier or a spouse or cohabitee with occupancy rights.

'Unlawful eviction' includes forcibly throwing the tenant out, as well as changing the locks.

'Harassment' is constituted by acts likely or calculated to interfere with the peace or comfort of the residential occupier by withdrawing services reasonably required for occupation of the premises. Examples include making threats against the tenant, disrupting gas, water or electricity supplies and moving in noisy neighbours.

Criminal prosecution

Anyone found guilty of unlawful eviction or harassment is liable to a fine or imprisonment or both.

Civil action for damages

The courts can award damages to tenants who have been unlawfully put out of their house. If a tenant gives up occupation of the premises because the landlord attempted to put him out of the house or indulged in conduct likely to cause the tenant to give up occupation of the premises, damages can also be awarded. Damages for unlawful destruction of the tenant's belongings can also be obtained.

The 1988 Act provides a formula for calculating these damages, which is the difference between the value of the landlord's interest in the property with the tenant in occupation and then with vacant possession at the time when the tenant was put or driven out.

LANDLORD'S DEFENCES

- if the landlord re-instates the tenant in the property before proceedings for damages are decided, or if the sheriff orders re-instatement, then no statutory damages will be payable. Re-instatement must be genuine – it is not enough simply to give the tenant the keys to re-gain access to a property which has been wrecked;
- genuine belief and reasonable cause to believe that the residential occupier has moved out, for example if the tenant has returned the keys or told the landlord he was moving on a particular day.

Sub-letting

You may sub-let part of the property if your tenancy agreement allows it. Generally, landlords specifically prohibit sub-letting in tenancy agreements. If the agreement is silent on the matter you can seek the landlord's consent.

PUBLIC SECTOR TENANCIES

These are known as 'secure tenancies' and are provided by land-lords which are one of the following bodies:

- a local authority;
- a development corporation;

- Scottish Homes;
- a registered housing association;
- a housing co-operative;
- a housing trust.

The tenant must be an individual and the property must be let as a separate dwelling.

The following types of tenancy are not secure tenancies:

- service tenancy/tied accommodation, i.e. where the tenant is an employee of the landlord and is required to occupy the house for the better performance of their duty;
- a temporary let to jobseekers;
- development and temporary letting, i.e. where the let expressly provides that it is temporary pending development of the property;
- decant property, i.e. property temporarily let to a secure tenant while work is being carried out to the tenant's own dwelling;
- homeless persons' temporary accommodation;
- agricultural and business premises;
- police and fire authority housing;
- houses which are part of or within the curtilage of certain other buildings, for example a janitor's house within school grounds.

Security of tenure

Generally this means the right to remain in the premises for the tenant's lifetime. Certain family members can also succeed to the tenancy on the death of the tenant. A secure tenancy can only be brought to an end in the following circumstances:

- death of a tenant where there is no 'qualified person' to succeed. A qualified person is the spouse, cohabitee or survivor of a joint tenancy where the property was the survivor's only or principal home at the time of the tenant's death. Alternatively, a qualified person can be a member of the tenant's family over the age of 16 where the property was that person's only or principal home throughout the 12 months immediately prior to the tenant's death;

- declining of the tenancy by a qualified person;

- death of a succeeding qualified person, i.e. where a qualified person succeeds to the tenancy and later dies;

- written agreement between the landlord and the tenant;

- abandonment of the tenancy. The landlord must have reasonable grounds for believing that the tenant had ceased to occupy the property. The landlord must serve certain notices and then can bring the tenancy to an end without further proceedings;

- possession order from the sheriff court. The landlord must serve notice on the tenant in the prescribed form, giving:

    – four weeks' notice; and

    – a statement of the ground on which possession is sought.

There are 16 grounds for possession. Grounds 1–7 have been described as the **conduct grounds**. Briefly, these are:

- when the rent is unpaid;

- another obligation under the tenancy is breached;

- using the property for immoral or illegal purposes;
- deterioration of the property or furniture;
- absence from the property without reasonable cause;
- obtaining the tenancy by false statements; and
- conduct which constitutes nuisance or annoyance.

The sheriff must make an order if one or more of the above grounds are established and it is reasonable to make the order.

Grounds 8–15 have been described as the **management grounds**. Briefly, these are:

- conduct which constitutes nuisance or annoyance and the landlord considers it appropriate to move the tenant to other accommodation;
- overcrowding;
- demolition or substantial works to the building;
- re-possession of a property designed or adapted for a person with special needs;
- re-possession of a property provided for a person needing special social support;
- re-possession of a property provided by a housing association for special categories for persons such as the aged or infirm;
- re-possession where the landlord's rights have ended;
- re-possession of a property required to provide accommodation for an education worker for a designated authority.

Ground 16 is transfer of the tenancy to a former spouse or cohabitee under the Matrimonial Homes (Family Protection) (Scotland) Act 1981.

Under Grounds 8–15 the sheriff **must** grant the order where the ground is established and other suitable housing will be made available to the tenant when the order takes effect. The court must look at whether the alternative accommodation provides equivalent security of tenure and reasonably meets the needs of the tenant and his family.

Right to buy

Local authority tenants have the statutory right to buy their houses under the Tenants' Rights, etc. (Scotland) Act 1980.

To qualify, the tenancy must be a secure tenancy of property which is let as a separate dwelling. The tenant must be an individual who occupies it as his only or principal home and the landlord must be one of the specific list of public sector land-lords.

The tenant must be a public sector tenant at the date of the application to purchase. The applicant need not have occupied the property which they are applying to purchase for two years, but must have been a public sector tenant for at least that period of time.

Price

The price is the market value of the property at a discount calculated on the basis of how long the tenant has been a tenant of a public sector landlord.

Discount

The discount on houses is 32 per cent of the market value, with an additional 1 per cent of the market value for every year of con-tinuous occupation beyond two, up to a maximum of 60 per cent

The discount on flats is 44 per cent of the market value, with an additional 2 per cent of the market value for every year of continuous occupation beyond two, up to a maximum of 70 per cent.

Repayment of discount

If the tenant sells the property within three years of purchase, the landlord can recover a proportion of the difference between the market value and the discounted purchase price. The proportions are 100 per cent where tenant sells the property in the first year after purchase, 66 per cent during the second year and 33 per cent during the third year. There is no recovery of the discount where the property is being sold by the executors of a deceased tenant or purchaser.

Financing the purchase

Local authorities are obliged under statute to provide loans to tenants wishing to exercise the right to buy. The amount of the loan must not exceed the price fixed for the property.

6 Setting Up Home

The urge to mate and create a secure home has driven us since pre-historic man banded together in caves for shelter. This instinct is at the very root of society and much of the law's work over the centuries has been focused on trying to regulate the way we live together or to resolve family disputes without bloodshed and feud. In this chapter we will examine how well modern Scots law has succeeded in these achieving these aspirations.

MARRIAGE

Who can get married?

The law stipulates that parties to a marriage must:

- be unmarried;
- be over the age of 16;
- be of the opposite sex to each other;
- not be closely related to each other;
- agree to the marriage (i.e. it must be a voluntary union).

Unmarried

The law regards you as a single person if:

- you have never been married at all; or
- you have been married but that marriage has been dissolved by recognised divorce proceedings or your spouse has died or the marriage has been annulled.

The first of these points is self-explanatory but the second needs some elaboration:

MARRIAGE ENDED BY DIVORCE

Divorce is recognised in Scotland if it is obtained in a Scottish court, according to Scots law. A divorce granted by a civil court elsewhere in the British Isles is also recognised in Scotland. A divorce obtained abroad is recognised provided that it took place according to the law of the country where it was granted and either party to the marriage was habitually resident in that country or domiciled there or a national of that country. A foreign divorce obtained otherwise and by means of proceedings (for example a Muslim 'talak' or Jewish 'get') may be recognised if certain requirements regarding domicile and habitual residence are met.

MARRIAGE ENDED BY DEATH OF A SPOUSE

In the vast majority of cases this is established simply by production of a death certificate. Where that cannot be done, for example if a spouse has simply disappeared or is believed to have died, the law allows you to obtain a **declarator of death** if the missing person is thought to have died or has not been known to be alive for at least seven years. If the circumstances of the missing person's disappearance point to death at or around a particular time, proceedings can be raised immediately after that point – in other words, you do not have to wait seven years. If there is no positive indication that the missing person has died but they have not been known to be alive for some time then court action can only be started seven years after the date on which the person was last known to be alive.

MARRIAGE ENDED BY DECLARATOR OF NULLITY OF MARRIAGE

See page 134.

POLYGAMOUS MARRIAGE

Polygamous unions are not recognised under Scots law. For example, if you marry a foreigner in Scotland and then discover that he already has a wife in his own country, where polygamous marriages are legal, your own marriage to him would be void under Scots law. In other words, the law in Scotland looks upon your marriage as having never taken place.

Age

Any single person domiciled in Scotland and aged over 16 can get married here. A marriage in Scotland between parties where either one is aged under 16 is void.

Marriage must be between parties of the opposite sex

Marriage in Scots law is a union between a man and a woman. A marriage between two parties of the same sex is **void**.
Transsexuals who wish to marry cannot do so because, even

though they have undergone a sex change in physical terms, for legal purposes their sex remains as it was on their birth certificate and cannot be changed.

No marriage can take place between close relations

The law prohibits marriage between persons in certain degrees of relationship. These can be divided into three categories:

- blood ties (consanguinity);
- marriage (affinity);
- adoption.

CONSANGUINITY

<u>A man cannot marry</u>	<u>A woman cannot marry</u>
His mother	Her father
His paternal grandmother	Her paternal grandfather
His maternal grandmother	Her maternal grandfather
His paternal great-grandmother	Her paternal great-grandfather
His maternal great-grandmother	Her maternal great-grandfather
His daughter	Her son
His granddaughter	Her grandson
His great granddaughter	Her great grandson
His sister	Her brother
His paternal aunt	Her paternal uncle
His maternal aunt	Her maternal uncle
His niece	Her nephew

First cousins are free to marry each other.

Affinity

A man cannot marry	**A woman cannot marry**
The daughter of his former wife	The son of her former husband
The granddaughter of his former wife	The grandson of her former husband
His father's former wife	Her mother's former husband
His grandfather's former wife	Her grandmother's former husband

Step-brothers and step-sisters can marry each other.

However, in all of the above cases of prohibition because of relationship by marriage, the parties may marry where both are over the age of 21 and the younger party to the marriage has not lived in the same household as the older party and been treated by him or her as a child of the family, at any time while he or she was under the age of 18.

It should also be noted that in certain exceptional circumstances former parents-in-law and children-in-law can marry each other.

Adoption

A man cannot marry	**A woman cannot marry**
His adoptive mother or former adoptive mother	Her adoptive father or former adoptive father
His adopted daughter or former adopted daughter	Her adopted son or former adopted son

Marriage must be voluntary

Marriage is a contract like any other and requires the parties to consent. A marriage will be invalid if either party did not truly consent to it. Lack of consent or defective consent can arise in the following circumstances:

- mental illness or defect;
- intoxication by drink or drugs at the time of the marriage ceremony;
- error;
- force and fear;
- sham marriages.

Marriages which are void or voidable

A void marriage is of no legal effect whatsoever. There is no need to obtain a court order to annul it, although in practical terms it may be necessary or desirable to obtain such an order. A marriage may be void on any of the following grounds:

- either of the parties was already married when the marriage was entered into;
- either of the parties was under the age of 16 when the marriage was entered into;
- the parties were of the same sex;
- the parties fall within the prohibited degrees of relationship;
- lack of consent.

A **voidable** marriage is valid until a court order called a **decree of declarator of nullity** is obtained. There is only one ground on which a marriage may be voidable in Scots law and that is the incurable impotency of one or both parties at the date of the marriage.

Engagement

The majority of couples still become engaged prior to marrying. An engagement used to be regarded as a contract under Scots law and if you broke off the engagement without good cause you could be sued for damages. This law was only abolished in 1984. The present position is that an engagement is no longer a legally enforceable contract in Scotland. You are perfectly entitled to break off an engagement and cannot be sued for doing so. A broken engagement can of course give rise to other difficulties, usually in connection with property issues.

Property of engaged couples

There is no specific law dealing with these matters between engaged couples. Instead they are covered by the general principles of the law of property and contract. Therefore, when an engagement is broken off each party is still the sole owner of whatever property he or she brought to the relationship. Items purchased jointly by the engaged couple are owned jointly and parties would be well advised simply to try to agree how such items should be divided between them on their separation.

The law on financial provision on divorce does not apply to engaged couples who split up before marriage. Where title to a house or flat has been taken equally in the names of both parties the law is that they have equal rights to the property and the proceeds of its sale. Where the title has been taken in the name of one party to the engagement but the other has expended money on the property, the second party may have the right to recover that money on the basis of **unjust enrichment** (see Glossary, p. 263). This could also apply where the property was in joint names but one party could prove that he or she provided the deposit or other funds spent on the property from his or her own resources.

The ring

Scots law does not make any specific provision in relation to the return of an engagement ring. Since there are no legal rights or obligations arising out of the engagement, it is arguable that the ring is an outright gift in the way that a Christmas or birthday present is and is therefore not returnable.

One can envisage a situation where the ring is a family heirloom from the groom's family, which he would wish to have returned if the marriage does not proceed. He could raise a court action to seek its return in those circumstances, on the basis that the ring was gifted in contemplation of marriage and that it would be unjust for his ex-fiancée to retain it when the marriage is not to proceed.

Wedding gifts

It is settled that if the marriage is not to proceed, an engaged couple must return wedding gifts to those who have given them.

Marriage formalities

There are two types of marriage ceremony in Scotland:

- a civil ceremony; and
- a religious ceremony.

There are certain preliminaries which must be gone through in advance of either type:

Marriage notices

Each party to the marriage must submit a marriage notice to the District Registrar in the Registration District where the marriage is to take place. This must be submitted with:

- a fee;
- the birth certificate of the party submitting it;
- the decree of divorce or declarator of nullity, where the party submitting the notice has been married before and the marriage has been dissolved;
- the death certificate of the former spouse, where the party submitting the notice is a widow or a widower.

These details are entered into the marriage notice book and the names of the parties and the proposed date of the marriage are displayed at the Registrar's office. Anyone wishing to submit an objection to an intended marriage must put it in writing to the District Registrar. If the objection is a serious one, for example that one of the parties is already married, then the matter must be reported by the District Registrar to the Registrar General of Scotland who must investigate it. The issue of the marriage schedule is suspended while this investigation is in progress.

The usual minimum waiting period between lodging of the marriage notice and a civil ceremony taking place or the issue of a marriage schedule for a religious ceremony to take place is 14 days. This is to enable objections to be made. The period can be reduced in certain circumstances.

Marriage schedule

This document is made up by the Registrar on expiry of the 14-day period. It contains the parties' details and is the licence which authorises the religious celebrant (e.g. minister, priest or rabbi) to proceed with a religious ceremony.

Civil ceremony

This usually takes place in the Registrar's office and is conducted by the Registrar during normal office hours. The Registrar keeps the marriage schedule until the date of the marriage. The Registrar can only conduct the ceremony outwith his office if:

- one of the parties cannot attend because of serious illness or serious bodily injury; and
- delay of the wedding is undesirable; and
- either party has notified the Registrar of this and asked for the ceremony to take place elsewhere within a Registration District, for example at a hospital.

Both parties must attend, and there must also be two witnesses over the age of 16. The parties must declare that:

- there are no legal impediments to their marriage; and
- they take each other as husband and wife.

They are then declared to be married and both parties, the two witnesses and the Registrar all sign the marriage schedule and the marriage is registered.

Religious ceremony

A religious ceremony can be carried out at any time and anywhere but the details must be specified in advance in the marriage schedule. The ceremony must be carried out by an authorised celebrant. In Scotland this is:

- a minister of the Church of Scotland; or

- a minister, clergyman, pastor, priest or other marriage celebrant of a religious body prescribed in regulations made by the Secretary of State; or

- a celebrant nominated by another religious body (e.g. Islam, Hindu).

The parties must produce the marriage schedule and both parties must be present, with two witnesses over the age of 16. Following the ceremony the parties, the witnesses and the celebrant sign the schedule, which must then be returned to the District Registration Office within three days of the ceremony to enable the marriage to be registered.

Marrying abroad

Combining a wedding and a honeymoon in an exotic foreign location is becoming increasingly popular. There are a number of specialist travel agencies which can arrange wedding ceremonies in any number of countries from Europe to the Far East. The brochures usually give very specific instructions about the documentation required for each country, as well as any residence requirements. Generally speaking, a marriage that is valid under the law of the country in which it has taken place is accepted as a legally binding and valid marriage in this country but only if the marriage is valid by the laws of this country also. Accordingly, if both parties live in Scotland but choose to marry abroad when one of them is under the age of 16 the marriage would be invalid (i.e. void under Scots law) even though it could be a valid marriage in the country in which it took place.

The effects of marriage

Marriage creates certain legal consequences for the parties, which affect many aspects of their lives.

Duty to live together

Spouses have a duty to live with one another. They can, of course, separate if the marriage becomes unhappy. Where a spouse leaves without reasonable cause and refuses to return that spouse is regarded as being in desertion (see Divorce, p. 210).

Duty to maintain

In Scots law this is known as the duty to aliment. Each party owes this duty toward the other. The duty is 'to provide such support as is reasonable in the circumstances'. The factors to be considered are:

- the needs and resources of the parties;
- the earning capacities of the parties;
- generally, all the circumstances of the case.

While the parties are living together the duty to maintain is usually of no great significance, being fulfilled by whatever domestic and financial arrangements the parties choose to make. Its significance arises on separation, as it is usually at that point that the duty to maintain has to be quantified in monetary terms.

Sexual relations

A sexual relationship between spouses is an accepted part of marriage. Refusal to consummate a marriage could give rise to divorce proceedings.

Sexual intercourse must be consensual. A husband can be charged with the rape of his wife if he forces himself upon her. This applies even where the couple are living together.

Fidelity

Spouses are expected to be faithful to each other. If a spouse voluntarily has sexual intercourse with a third party while married this constitutes adultery and could give rise to an action of divorce (see Divorce, p. 207).

Name

Many women take their husband's surname on marriage but they are not obliged to do so. A woman can continue to use her husband's surname after his death or after divorce. Equally, she can revert to her maiden name. There are no formalities for any such change of name. A bride-to-be can apply for a British passport in her married name before the wedding. The passport will be postdated with the married name. Application for this must be made on forms obtainable from the Passport Agency.

A husband can use his wife's surname or the couple can use both surnames together.

Matrimonial property

Again, this is an issue which generally acquires significance only on separation or divorce. In Scots law there is a presumption that a couple's household goods are owned in common. Money, securities, motor vehicles and pets are not classed as household goods so the presumption of joint ownership does not apply to them. Savings made from housekeeping money are, in the absence of agreement to the contrary, presumed to belong to the couple in equal shares. For the purposes of divorce, matrimonial property is specifically defined (see Divorce, p. 221). Broadly speaking, it includes the matrimonial home and furnishings (even if these were acquired before the marriage, as long as they were acquired by the couple for use as a family home and contents) and all other assets acquired by the parties in the course of the marriage other than by way of gift or inheritance from a third party. The courts have extensive powers to re-distribute assets between husband and wife on divorce.

Matrimonial home

Irrespective of whether the matrimonial home is owned or tenant-ed in joint names or in the name of only one spouse, a spouse has the right to occupy the matrimonial home and not to be excluded from it (see Divorce, p. 232).

GRANTING SECURITY OVER THE MATRIMONIAL HOME

Nowadays it is very common for the matrimonial home to be owned in the joint names of the couple. In recent years there have been a number of court cases in England and Scotland where one spouse (usually the husband) has persuaded the other to use the matrimonial home as security for him to obtain a loan for his business. In that situation, if the husband defaults on the loan repayments the bank can call up its security and re-possess the house in satisfaction of the loan.

A spouse who is asked to allow the matrimonial home to be used as security for the other spouse's business debts must take independent legal advice. The courts have recognised that in these circumstances many women are vulnerable to their husband's influence. For such a loan to be valid, the court would have to be satisfied that:

- the wife is consenting to giving the home as security freely and of her own choice;

- she understands the nature of the loan agreement;

- the transaction is one into which she would be sensibly advised to enter.

Where banks and other lenders are asked to draw up security documents for this sort of loan they are under a duty to insist that the wife seeks independent legal advice before signing the documentation.

Parenthood

Husband and wife have equal parental rights and responsibilities in relation to the children of their marriage. Either can exercise those rights and responsibilities without consulting the other. These rights and responsibilities include matters such as the child's religion, education and consent to medical treatment, etc.

On separation or divorce, the court can be asked to alter the relationship between parent and child, for example by ordering that the child should reside primarily with one parent or by depriving a parent of some or all of his or her parental rights and responsibilities. Both parents have a continuing obligation to maintain the children of the marriage after divorce (see Divorce, p. 218 and Children, p. 177).

Tax position of husband and wife

At the time of writing, a married couple are entitled to a married couple's allowance, which is transferable between them. Each of them is entitled to the single person's tax allowance and they can then elect which of them should receive the married couple's allowance. The married couple's allowance is, however, to be abolished with effect from 6 April 2000 and replaced with a children's tax credit. This means that married couples will generally be placed on the same footing as unmarried couples for the purposes of income tax.

Gifts between husband and wife are not liable to capital gains tax.

On the death of your spouse, if you inherit under your spouse's will you are entitled to take your share of the estate free of inheritance tax (for further information see Death, p. 245).

Nationality

Marriage does not affect nationality, to the extent that you retain the nationality you had before you were married. The foreign spouse of a British citizen can acquire citizenship by naturalisation.

Marriage is of considerable importance in relation to immigration. Different rules apply, depending on whether you are:

- a British citizen or Commonwealth citizen with the right of abode;
- a national of a Member State of the European Economic Area or a family member of such a national;
- neither of the above.

A detailed discussion of these matters is beyond the scope of this book. If you are in any doubt regarding nationality issues you must seek expert legal advice.

A U.K. resident can bring his or her spouse into the U.K. if the following conditions are satisfied:

- the parties to the marriage have met;
- each intends to live permanently with the other and the marriage is continuing;
- they have adequate accommodation for themselves and their dependants in accommodation which they own or occupy exclusively and can afford without help from public funds;
- they can maintain themselves and their dependants adequately without help from public funds;
- the applicant holds valid U.K. entry clearance for entry in the capacity of spouse. Similar rules apply to fiancé(e)s.

Immigration law is intended in part to prevent bogus marriages of convenience to U.K. residents, which are intended to get round the strict immigration laws. To obtain an entry clearance certificate to enter the U.K. as a fiancé(e) or as a spouse you will have to satisfy the immigration authorities that:

- your 'primary purpose' is to get married;
- you and your spouse intend to live together as man and wife;
- if you are entering the U.K. as a fiancé(e), the marriage will take place within six months. You must also show that you intend to settle in the U.K.

LIVING TOGETHER

It is a popular misconception that couples who live together but

145

are not married are 'common law husband and wife'. The law of Scotland, common or otherwise, does not actually recognise such a concept.

There is the concept, unique to Scots law, of marriage by cohabitation with habit and repute. If this can be established it gives the parties the status of a regular marriage with all the rights and obligations that that entails. To prove marriage by cohabitation with habit and repute you must establish the following:

- the couple live together as husband and wife in Scotland;
- the period of living together must be sufficiently long for the court to infer that the parties tacitly agreed to marry;
- the parties must be reputed to be husband and wife. In other words, they must be regarded by family, friends and society in general to be nothing other than husband and wife;
- the parties must have legal capacity to marry (see p. 129).

It should be appreciated from this that marriage by cohabitation by habit and repute is a concept quite distinct from that of ordinary cohabitation.

In the main, the law regards a cohabiting couple as two single people.

No legal duties

While cohabiting couples may have a moral duty to care for, support and be faithful to one another, the law does not impose those duties upon them, nor does it do so when they separate.

No duty to cohabit

Either party can leave at any time to cohabit with or marry

someone else without having to go through any formal legal procedures whatsoever.

No duty to maintain

There is no duty on cohabitees to maintain or aliment each other. There is no law which provides for adjustment of assets between the parties on separation to ensure that each receives adequate financial provision. Thus, a woman who cohabits with a man in his home and who is maintained by him from his earnings has no claim on any of these assets if the relationship fails. This is in marked contrast to the legal remedies available to a spouse on divorce.

On separation cohabitees still have a legally enforceable obligation to maintain the children of the relationship (see Children, p. 177).

Parenthood

Parental rights and responsibilities in relation to a child whose parents are not married lie solely with the mother. Under the Children (Scotland) Act 1995 the father can acquire parent rights and responsibilities if he and the mother agree to enter into a parental rights and parental responsibilities agreement. This can only happen if the mother has not been deprived of any of her parental responsibilities. You must complete and register a prescribed form (see Children, p. 155). Once the agreement is made it cannot be revoked by the parents but only by court order. If the mother will not be party to such an agreement then the father can apply to the court for an order for parental rights and parental responsibilities. (see Children, p.155).

Buying a home together

If a cohabiting couple purchase a property and their contributions to the purchase price are in anything other than equal proportions they should obtain legal advice to ensure that the title to the property or a written agreement on future sale proceeds reflects that unequal contribution. Failure to do so can lead to disputes over division of the proceeds if the property is sold. If one party provides the whole of the deposit or offers to pay more than half of the mortgage and expects that greater contribution to be reflected in the division of the sale proceeds then there should be a written agreement to that effect (see Engagement, p. 135).

Protection from domestic violence

Certain aspects of the legislation which is designed to protect spouses from domestic violence are extended to cohabiting couples. At present this covers only heterosexual cohabiting couples. Its provisions usually become relevant only when a relationship is breaking down and the partner in whose name the house is owned or tenanted tries to force the other out. In that situation, if you are cohabiting with your partner in a house either solely owned or solely rented by them you can ask the court to grant you the right to occupy the house for an initial period not exceeding six months. You can get further extensions of this period. The court must consider how long you have been living together and whether there are children of the relationship. Once occupancy rights are granted, or where you are the joint tenant or joint owner of the property, the following provisions apply, with certain restrictions:

- the rights to make payments (e.g. mortgage, endowment

premiums, hire purchase) and effect repairs to the property and to seek a court order sharing liability for these bills between you, or if you have no income ordering your cohabitee to pay them;

- the right to seek enforcement of your occupancy rights and the restriction of your cohabitee's occupancy rights;
- exclusion order;
- transfer of tenancy;
- interdict and power of arrest (see Divorce, p. 235).

Tax

Cohabitees and married couples are in broadly similar positions for the purposes of income tax. There are, however, still important differences between the positions of a married couple and a cohabiting couple in other areas of taxation, for example:

- gifts between husband and wife are free of capital gains tax but gifts between cohabiting couples are not;
- if a cohabitee inherits the estate of his or her cohabitee on that person's death, the estate is subject to inheritance tax. Where spouses inherit from each other they do so free of inheritance tax.

Death

A cohabitee has no **right** to inherit if the other cohabitee dies intestate, i.e. without making a will. It is essential that cohabitees should make wills providing for each other if that is what they wish to happen on their respective deaths. Verbal expression of that intent or informal writings will not be enough. Cohabitees have no rights to a widow's pension or a widowed mother's allowance. Under company pension schemes the trustees of the scheme have discretion to allow a cohabitee to be a beneficiary. Spouses benefit automatically. If you want your cohabitee to benefit under your company pension scheme you must check with the scheme administrators if they will accept your nomination of him or her as the beneficiary.

Nationality

A cohabitee has no **right** to bring a foreign partner into this country.

Names

There is nothing to prevent you from being known by your partner's surname. The concept of deed poll does not exist in Scots law. You simply start using your partner's surname. If you wish to use the name on certain official documents, such as a passport, then you will require to give a statutory declaration that you have been known by that name for a certain period of time. This declaration must be sworn before a solicitor. You must understand that even if you describe yourself as your partner's 'wife' or 'common law wife' or 'husband' or 'common law husband' these terms have no meaning in law and do not confer the rights of husband or wife upon you.

Where the law does treat cohabitees as husband and wife

We have seen above how the law treats a husband and wife differently from a cohabiting couple. There are, however, some areas where they are treated in the same way:

- the law in relation to domestic violence applies to cohabiting couples as well as spouses with certain restrictions (see Divorce, p. 237);

- cohabitees and husbands and wives can succeed to secure or assured tenancies;
- certain social security benefits are available for live-in couples as well as for parents and children, irrespective of marital status;
- cohabitees and husbands and wives have a duty to maintain the children of their relationship;
- cohabitees who are asked to use their home to secure the business debts of a partner are vulnerable to the same pressures as spouses, so the same safeguards should apply;
- for the purposes of assessing means under the legal aid rules, a partner's income will be taken into account in the same way as a spouse's will.

Some countries have enacted legislation to regulate the financial and other consequences of the breakdown of cohabiting couples' relationships. There is no such legislation in Scotland. Cohabiting couples may wish to consider creating their own agreements to deal with this situation. While this is theoretically possible there are several practical and legal considerations which militate against it. Few couples in the first flush of romance will feel inclined to enter into hard-headed discussion about the financial and other consequences of the breakdown of their relationship. Indeed such discussions themselves could lead to the end of the relationship there and then. Separating spouses successfully use separation agreements drawn up at the time of their separation, which are essentially contracts regulating the consequences of marital breakdown. However these are successful because there is legislation regulating that breakdown (i.e. divorce law) and the agreements draw their framework from that legislation. There is no legislative framework for cohabiting couples and therefore there would be scope for disputes over interpretation of the terms of any agreement made by them. In addition, it would be almost impossible to foresee all the eventualities which might arise over the period of a relationship. When a cohabiting couple's relationship does break down, if there is goodwill between them then they can agree to effect a fair distribution of assets. That can only work where they are able to reach agreement, however; where there is no agreement the couple are thrown back on the ordinary law of property and contract.

7 Children

PARENTHOOD

Who are a child's parents?

Legally, a child's **mother** is the woman who gives birth to the child. This is so even where the child is conceived from an egg donated by another woman. The mother of that child is the woman who carried and gave birth to it albeit that she and the child are not genetically related.

Establishing **fatherhood**, on the other hand, is a matter of biology in that, with certain exceptions, the child's father is defined as the man whose semen fertilised the egg, leading to the child's conception. The only exceptions are where the child is conceived by artificial insemination by donor (A.I.D.). Where a married woman conceives by A.I.D. her husband is presumed to be the father of the child, unless he has not consented to the treatment. Where cohabitees conceive by A.I.D. the man is presumed for all purposes to be the child's father where the treatment has been provided for him and his female partner together.

A man is presumed to be the father of a child if he was married to the child's mother at any time from the child's conception until its birth. A man will also be presumed to be the father of a child, where he is not married to the mother, if both he and the mother acknowledge that he is the father and name him as the father on the child's birth certificate. This can be done whether or not the couple are actually living together.

These are all simply legal presumptions which can be disproved. So, for example, if a married man believes that he is not the father of his wife's child he can ask the court to grant a declarator of non-parentage. Similarly, a woman whose boyfriend refuses to acknowledge that he is the father of her child can apply for a declarator of parentage.

Nowadays D.N.A. testing is the most common form of e vidence used to establish parentage or non-parentage. Samples of bodily fluid or tissue are taken from the child, the mother and the alleged or presumed father and D.N.A. 'fingerprinting' or 'profiling' can establish positively whether or not the man is the child's father. In most cases parties will consent to these tests. Any woman with parental responsibility for a child under the age of 16 can consent to a sample being taken from the child for the purposes of the test. This is usually done by taking a scraping of cells from the inside of the child's cheek, which is a less intrusive procedure than drawing a blood sample. The court may request the party to a parentage action to provide a sample or to consent to a sample being taken from a child but cannot **make** the person give such a sample or such consent. Refusal to give a sample or to consent to a sample being taken from a child can justify the inference that the person refusing may be hiding the truth.

Over the years the law has gradually eroded many of the significant differences which used to exist between the status of legitimate and illegitimate children. Where once it was thought that the advantage for a child of continuing to be considered legitimate could outweigh knowing the truth about his or her paternity, the modern view is that it will always be in the interests of the parents that the truth of a child's paternity be known, and usually in the interests of the child also.

Who has parental rights and responsibilities?

Mothers and married fathers

A child's mother **automatically** has parental rights and responsibilities, as does the father but only if he is or was married to the mother at the date of the child's conception or at any time thereafter.

Unmarried fathers

Unmarried fathers do not automatically have parental rights and responsibilities. They can **acquire** them by either:

- entering into an **agreement** with the child's mother to give the father the parental rights and responsibilities he would have had had they been married. The mother must have full parental rights and responsibilities herself in order to enter into this agreement. It must be a written agreement in a specified form and must be registered in the Books of Council and Session. The agreement cannot be cancelled except by court order; or

- where the mother will not agree to give the father parental rights and responsibilities in this manner the father can apply

to the court for an **order** for parental rights and responsibilities. In deciding whether to grant the order the welfare of
the child is the court's paramount consideration and it will
grant the order only if it is in the child's interests to do so.

Other parties

The legislation is drawn widely so that any person having an
interest can apply to the court for an order for parental rights and
responsibilities. Generally this will arise where a child has been
placed in the long-term care of other relatives, such as grandparents, or where a step-parent wishes to be put on an equal footing
with a natural parent. As mentioned above, the child's welfare is
the paramount consideration in deciding whether to grant the
order sought.

Those acting in place of a parent

Often parents leave children in the care of others, such as family
members, neighbours, friends or childminders. Children may go
on holiday with friends and their parents or be cared for by a
relative while a parent is in hospital. What is the carer's position?
They do not have parental rights and responsibilities. What they
do have is the responsibility to do what is reasonable in all the
circumstances to safeguard the child's health, development and
welfare.

This specifically includes the right to consent to surgical, medical or dental treatment on behalf of the child but only where:

- the child itself does not have legal capacity to consent (see p.
  162); and

- the carer has no reason to believe that the child's parent would refuse to consent.

The responsibility does not extend to teachers or others caring for a child at school.

Guardians

A guardian is a 'parent substitute' who has full parental rights and responsibilities in relation to a child. A guardian can be appointed by a child's parent or by the court. A guardian can also appoint a person to be the child's guardian in the event of the first guardian's death.

The appointment must be:

- in writing; and
- signed by the parent.

Most commonly it will be included in the parent's will. Appointing a guardian is a major decision and the views of the child and any other person with parental rights and responsibilities must be sought and considered in the making of the appointment. If, however, the child's or other parent's views are not sought or are ignored this does not mean that the appointment can be challenged.

The appointment is only effective where the person named as guardian accepts it. Where there is a guardian and a surviving parent they both have parental rights and responsibilities and each can exercise their parental rights without the consent of the other. Guardianship continues until the child becomes 18 or the guardian dies or the guardianship is terminated by the court.

What are parental rights and responsibilities?

Rights

In order to fulfil his parental responsibilities a parent has the right to:

- have the child live with them or otherwise decide where the child should live;
- control, direct or guide the child's upbringing;
- if the child does not live with the parent, to maintain personal relations and direct contact with the child on a regular basis;
- act as the child's legal representative.

Responsibilities

A parent has the responsibility to:

- safeguard and promote the child's health, development and welfare;
- provide direction and guidance to the child in a manner appropriate to the child's age and development;
- if the child is not living with the parent, to maintain personal relations and direct contact with the child on a regular basis;
- act as the child's legal representative.

Parental rights and responsibilities continue until the child is 16, with the exception of the parental responsibility to give guidance, which continues until the child is 18. Parental rights and responsibilities must be exercised only in the interests of the child. It will be seen that these rights and responsibilities are wide-ranging enough to cover all aspects of a child's life, such as:

- where and with whom a child is to live;
- social development;
- healthcare;
- education;
- religious upbringing;
- discipline;
- protection from harm; and
- management of property.

Failure to fulfil parental rights and responsibilities could amount to the criminal offence of neglect.

Child's views

When reaching any major decision involving parental rights or responsibilities, a parent must have regard to the views of the child, taking account of the child's age and maturity. The child is not obliged to give their views and even if they do the parent is not obliged to follow them. The law presumes that a child aged 12 or more is able to form and express a view but younger children who can do so should also be listened to where appropriate.

Specific parental rights and responsibilities

Residence

In the vast majority of households children do live with their parents in the exercise of this particular parental right and responsibility. It generally becomes an issue only when family life breaks down and a dispute arises about where and with whom the children should live (see p. 166). In most, but not all, situations a child will benefit from living with a parent or parents. As with all parental rights and responsibilities, however, it must be in the best interests of the child to do so.

Contact

This is the short name given to the right to maintain personal relations and direct contact with a child on a regular basis. This has replaced the previous concept of 'access'. The law is based on the assumption that it is of benefit to a child to continue to have links with both parents. By definition the right and responsibility of contact arise only when parents are no longer living together. Again, this right must be exercised on the basis of what is in the child's best interests and the child's views should be given appropriate weight.

Name

Parents have the right and responsibility to name a child. It is customary for the child of married parents to take the father's surname, although there is no legal obligation to do so. If a cohabiting couple wish to give the child the father's surname they must register the birth together, whereas either one of a married couple can register the birth alone, on production of the couple's marriage certificate.

CHANGING A CHILD'S NAME

Scots law, unlike English law, places little real legal significance on the name on the child's birth certificate because a person in Scotland may use a name by which he or she is known without any legal formality. Changing a child's name on a birth certificate is not, therefore, of great importance because a parent has the power to have a child known by a particular name simply by the use of that name. A change of name can be registered on the birth certificate but only on the application of both parents where they both have parental rights and responsibilities or on the application of one parent if only one has them. This provision is little used as generally the wish to change a child's name arises after separation or divorce. The typical situation will be where a woman re-marries or assumes the name of her new cohabitee and wishes the child of her previous relationship to have that name also. Where the natural father has parental rights and responsibilities the birth certificate cannot be changed without his consent, and in such cases that consent is unlikely to be forthcoming.

Usually what will happen is that the child will be known by the new surname anyway for all practical purposes as the mother is in a position to register that name with the school, doctor,-dentist, etc. The child's view should be taken into account.

The court could be asked to decide the matter on the application of either the parent who seeks to change the name, the parent who wishes it to remain as it is, or the child. The court would base its decision on what is in the child's best interests.

Discipline

This is an aspect of the parental right to control a child. A parent may physically chastise a child but the chastisement must be reasonable. The force used must be moderate. If it can be inferred from the severity of the parent's conduct that they intended to injure the child rather than punish them then the parent could be convicted of the criminal offence of cruelty.

Teachers in local authority schools cannot administer corporal punishment to pupils. Teachers in independent (private) schools can do so but the punishment must not amount to inhuman or degrading treatment.

Medical treatment

Parents have the responsibility to safeguard and promote the child's health and the right to consent to or refuse medical treatment on the child's behalf. The parent must exercise this right on the basis of what is in the child's best interests.

PARENT REFUSING TREATMENT

What if a parent refuses treatment which doctors consider necessary for the welfare of a child? For example, parents may refuse an essential blood transfusion on the ground that their religion does not allow the procedure. Parental refusal to consent to treatment could be overturned by the court in that situation, on the basis that they are not exercising their parental right in accordance with what is in the child's best interests.

CHILD'S OWN CHOICES

A child under 16 has capacity to consent to any surgical, medical or dental procedure if, in the opinion of the doctor or dentist attending the child, the child is capable of understanding the nature and possible consequences of the procedure or treatment. Essentially this means that a child could have such treatment without the parent's knowledge or consent. A common example of this would be where a teenage girl seeks a prescription for contraceptives.

Emigration, nationality and passport matters

EMIGRATION

Parents can decide jointly if a child should live with one or other
or both of them outwith the U.K. Removal of the child from the
U.K. by one parent without the consent of the other where they
both have parental rights and responsibilities is unlawful. This
can apply to short periods, such as holidays, as well as to permanent removal. The law does not lay down any specific procedure
for parental consent to take a child abroad but it is probably
advisable to get it in writing. If the other parent will not consent
you will have to ask the court to make an order allowing the child
to go (called a specific issue order – see below). The court's decision will be based on what is in the child's best interests.

NATIONALITY AND PASSPORT

A child born in the U.K. to married parents is automatically a
British citizen, provided that at the time of the birth one or both
of the parents is a British citizen or is settled in the U.K. without
time limit restriction. A child must now have their own passport
instead of being included on either parent's passport. A passport
application for a child can be made by either parent, where they
both have parental rights and responsibilities, or by any other
person who has parental rights and responsibilities for the child.

Religion

Parents have the right to choose a child's religion or to raise them
as a non-believer. The right to choose the child's religion must be
exercised in accordance with what is in the child's best interests. If

they cannot agree on the matter, parents can seek a specific issue order from the court to determine in which faith a child should be raised.

Legal representative

Usually a parent or other person entitled to act as the child's legal representative will enter into contracts or otherwise act on a child's behalf (for example, in bringing a court case for a child). A child under 16 can, however, enter into a transaction of a kind usually entered into by a child of that age, provided that the terms of the transaction are not unreasonable. For example, relatively young children have legal capacity, in transactions such as the purchase of sweets or comics, as those are transactions of a kind that a child of that age could be expected to enter into. The terms of the transaction must not be unreasonable if the child is to be bound by them. A child aged 12 or over can make a will and a child under 16 can instruct a solicitor to act for them in any civil court case, provided that the child has a general understanding of what it means to do so.

WHEN PARENTS SPLIT UP

The effect on parental rights and responsibilities

When married parents separate both continue to have parental rights and responsibilities in relation to their children. The position is the same for a cohabiting couple where the father has acquired parental rights and responsibilities by agreement or court order (see p. 155).

N.B. – Unmarried fathers who have not acquired parental

rights and responsibilities during the course of a relationship can do so on or after separation by application to the court.

The intention of the current legislation is that even after separation parents should still be left to regulate matters relating to their children and that the court should become involved only where absolutely necessary. This is called the 'minimum intervention principle'. So if you and your estranged spouse or cohabitee are able to agree between you where and with whom the children will live, contact arrangements for seeing the other parent and on-going communication about health, education, etc., you do not have to have a court order to regulate these matters. This is, of course, subject to what you decide being in the child's best interests. If you wish, you can set out your agreement in writing in a **minute of agreement** or simply discuss the matter and agree it between you verbally. If you need help in sorting out such an agreement you should consult a solicitor or local family mediation service. If you cannot agree and have to go to court the sheriff can also order you to attend **mediation** (see Divorce, p. 203).

Court orders regulating parental rights and responsibilities

These orders are only necessary where separating parents cannot agree on the arrangements for the children or where a third party seeks an order in relation to a child. The orders are made under section 11 of the Children (Scotland) Act 1995. The three main principles of the Act are:

- the welfare of the child will be the paramount consideration in decisions on the child's future;

- the minimum intervention principle, i.e. an order should be made in relation to a child only when the court is sure that to do so is better for the child than making no order at all;

- regard should be had to the child's view. The court must give the child a chance to say whether they want to express a view about any order which might be made. If the child does want to express a view the court must arrange for their views to be taken. The court must pay attention to the child's views, taking account of their age and maturity, but only in so far as the views are consistent overall with the child's best interests. A child over the age of 12 is deemed capable of forming and expressing a view. A child under 12 can form and express a view and the court can take account of that. A child should not be pressurised into giving a view. Parents should be very careful not to misinterpret this requirement and give the child the impression that they must decide who they want to live with or whether they want to see the other parent. This places an intolerable burden on a child and is not the intention of the legislation. If a child wishes to express a view the parent should make it clear to them that their view will help the judge to decide but it will not be the only thing the judge takes into account.

Orders the court can make

RESIDENCE ORDER

This is an order to decide with whom the child should live. Where someone who is not the child's parent is awarded a residence order (e.g. grandparents) the order also gives them parental rights and responsibilities. The court takes many factors into account in deciding with which parent a child should reside. Each case turns on its own facts but some factors which are likely to be relevant are:

- personality and character of each parent and the child's relationship with each of them;

- stability and continuity of care. In the main, the longer a child remains in the care of one parent the less keen the court will be to disturb that arrangement unless there are very good reasons for so doing;

- the desirability for babies and young children to have the care of their mother;

- the need to keep brothers and sisters together;

- the child's views.

CONTACT ORDER

This is an order providing that the person with whom the child lives must allow the child to spend time with the person named in the order or allow other contact such as exchange of letters or telephone calls. This is most common where parents split up and the children continue to reside with one but not the other. The courts generally accept that it is in the child's best interests to maintain contact with both parents unless there is evidence to show that this is not so. If you are being refused contact with your child you should act promptly to try to restore the bond. If reasoning and negotiation with your ex-partner fail, try suggesting mediation, failing which you should consult a solicitor with a view to seeking an agreement or raising court proceedings.

SPECIFIC ISSUE ORDER

This is an order to decide specific questions which have arisen in the child's upbringing, for example change of name, consent or refusal to medical treatment or consent to take a child abroad for a holiday or to live permanently.

INTERDICT

This is an order prohibiting any steps specified in the order being taken in relation to the child or their property, for example taking a child abroad, consenting to medical treatment which is not in the child's best interests or selling property belonging to a child.

OTHER ORDERS

The court can also make orders:

- depriving someone of some or all of their parental rights or parental responsibilities;
- imposing parental rights and responsibilities on someone who does not have them (for example, an unmarried father);
- appointing a judicial factor to manage a child's property;
- appointing or removing a person as guardian of a child (see p. 157).

The court can make these orders in proceedings raised specifically for the purpose or as part of other proceedings, for example divorce. Any person claiming an interest can apply for the orders. This is wide-ranging and covers natural parents, step-parents, other relatives or individuals involved in the child's care. A health authority could apply for the right to consent to medical treatment on behalf of a child whose parents are refusing to consent.

A child itself can apply for an order, for example if they are unhappy at home and want to live with grandparents. In these circumstances a child is entitled to have their own solicitor and can obtain legal aid.

EDUCATION

Parents' duty to educate

The law requires parents to ensure that their children receive a suitable education from the ages of five to 16. The parents have a duty to ensure that the child attends school unless they are providing appropriate education by other means, for example at home or at a private school. The duty to educate a child is an aspect of the parental responsibility to promote the child's development and provide direction and guidance. The education must be suitable to the child's age, ability and aptitude.

Once a child is enrolled in a public (i.e. State) school their attendance there is compulsory unless the education authority has consented to their withdrawal. If the child fails to attend school regularly the parent is guilty of a criminal offence, unless there is reasonable excuse for it, for example prolonged ill health. A parent may also avoid liability under the criminal law where it is physically impossible for the parent to compel the child's attendance, for example where a parent is suffering from an illness which makes him incapable of making the child attend or where a physically mature teenage child simply refuses to attend.

A parent cannot elect to have a child educated partly within the State system and partly outwith, for example by sending the child to State school for part of the school day and arranging private tuition in certain subjects for the remainder of the day.

School discipline

Corporal punishment is not permitted in State schools. It is permitted in independent or private schools but it must not be inhuman or degrading.

Exclusion of a pupil

An education authority may exclude a child from school if it considers that:

- the pupil's parent is refusing or failing to comply or is refusing or failing to allow the pupil to comply with the rules, regulations or disciplinary requirements of the school; or
- in all the circumstances the child's continued attendance at the school is likely to be seriously detrimental to order and discipline in the school or the educational wellbeing of the pupils there.

It will be seen that the first point relates to the child itself whereas the second also covers the wellbeing of the other pupils.

REVIEW OF EXCLUSION

The parents may appeal the decision to exclude to an appeal committee which can confirm or overturn the decision. If the child has been excluded until certain conditions have been met the committee may confirm the exclusion but modify the conditions. The committee's decision and the reasons for it must be given in writing to the parents and the education authority. The parents, but not the education authority, have a further right of appeal from the appeal committee to the sheriff court in the district where the school is situated. Both the appeal committee and the sheriff must, when considering the appeal, consider whether there were grounds for exclusion as set out above and whether the decision to exclude was reasonable in the circumstances.

Education authority's duty to provide education

It is the duty of every education authority to provide adequate and sufficient education to every child living within its area. The duty includes the duty to provide 'special education' for pupils whose physical, intellectual, emotional or social development is such that ordinary methods of education do not meet their needs.

Parental choice

The Education (Scotland) Act 1980 provides that pupils are to be educated in accordance with the wishes of their parents but only in so far as this is compatible with the provision of suitable instruction and training and the avoidance of unreasonable expenditure of public funds. The education authority must produce information about its arrangements for placing children in its schools. The authority will place a child in the school for the catchment area in which it lives and must inform the parents of that decision and of the parents' right to make a placing request, if they wish the child to attend another school under the management of the education authority.

Placing request

A parent can make a written request to an education authority to place their child in a particular school specified in the request.

The education authority must place the child in that school unless:

- doing so would:
  - make it necessary for the education authority to employ an additional teacher;
  - involve costly extensions or alterations to the school building or its facilities;
  - be seriously detrimental to the continuity of the child's education;
  - be likely to be seriously detrimental to order and discipline in the school;
  - be likely to be seriously detrimental to the educational well-being of pupils at the school;
- the education normally provided at the school is not suited to the child's age, ability or aptitude;
- the education authority has already required the child to stop attending that school; or
- the school is a special school and the child does not have special educational needs which would be covered at that school, or
- the school is a single-sex school and the child is not of the appropriate sex; or
- the child lives outwith the catchment area of the school and acceptance of the placing request would prevent the education authority from retaining reserved places at the school for pupils likely to move into the catchment area in the academic year during which the placing request is made.

The authority must inform the parent in writing of its decision on a placing request. Where the placing request is refused the decision must give reasons and inform the parent of the right to appeal to the appeal committee.

Appeal

An appeal to the appeal committee must be lodged with 28 days of the parent receiving the education authority's decision on the placing request. An appeal can be received late if there is a good excuse for the lateness. There can be only one appeal in relation to a child within any 12-month period.

The appeal committee must confirm the education authority's decision if:

- it is satisfied that one or more of the grounds of refusal above exists; and
- in all the circumstances it is appropriate to confirm the decision.

If it is not satisfied on the first two points above it must require the authority to grant the placing request. The decision must be given in writing to both the parent and the education authority and must give reasons. Where the authority's decision is confirmed the parent must be advised of their right of appeal to the sheriff court. The education authority has no such right of appeal.

Appeal to the sheriff court

Again, this must be made within 28 days of receiving the appeal committee's decision although a late appeal can be allowed if there is a good excuse. The sheriff must apply the same test to the appeal committee's decision as the appeal committee must apply to the educational authority's decision (see p. 171). The sheriff's decision is final.

Religious education

State schools must provide religious education but must be open to pupils of all religious denominations. A pupil can be withdrawn from religious education classes or religious assembly or worship by their parents.

Private sector

In private schools the relationship between the parent and the school is a matter of the contract between them. This will set out the fees, syllabus, discipline, etc.

THE CHILD SUPPORT AGENCY

Parents, whether married or unmarried, have a legal obligation to maintain their child. The Child Support Act 1991 largely deprived the courts of the right to fix the amount of child maintenance and govern the procedures for its recovery. Instead the Act placed these tasks in the hands of the Child Support Agency (C.S.A.) which is run by the Department of Social Security.

Who is covered by the Child Support Agency?

Qualifying child

A child qualifies for maintenance under the Child Support Act if he is:

under the age of 16; or

aged 16–18 and in full-time non-advanced education; or

aged 16–17 and registered for work or youth training; and

one or both of their parents is or are absent parents (see below).

Absent parent

An absent parent is a parent who is not living at home with their child and the child has their home with a person with care (see below).

Person with care

This is the person with whom the qualifying child has his home. This can, of course, be a parent but could also be someone else, for example a grandparent or a step-parent.

The Act applies only where the qualifying child, the absent parent and the person with care are all habitually resident in the U.K. The courts still have the right to deal with cases where the absent parent or the person with care lives abroad.

Who <u>must</u> apply to the Child Support Agency?

A person with care who is a parent of the qualifying child **must** apply to the C.S.A. where they are receiving income support or income-based jobseeker's allowance. This is so even where that parent had a pre-existing court order or maintenance agreement.

Who <u>may</u> apply to the Child Support Agency?

- parents who are persons with care who are not receiving income support or income-based jobseeker's allowance;

- any person with care who is not the parent of the qualifying child, for example a grandparent or step-parent. People within either of the last two categories can avoid the C.S.A. altogether and make a voluntary agreement with the other person or persons who is or are liable to maintain the child;

- a qualifying child aged 12 or over, provided that neither the person with care nor the absent parent has made an application.

If under any of these three points there is already a written maintenance agreement entered into **before** 5 April 1993 or a pre-existing court order, that prevents an application being made to the C.S.A. The parties to such an agreement or court order still have the right to go to court to have it altered on any material change in circumstances. Where there is a written agreement on maintenance, any clause which claims to prevent either party to the agreement from applying to the C.S.A. is not effective.

A written agreement on maintenance entered into **on or after** 5 April 1993 can also be varied downwards or terminated on a material change in circumstances by application to the court.

The making of a child maintenance assessment by the C.S.A. constitutes a material change in circumstances that would allow you to apply to the court for a downward variation or termination of such an agreement. If the parties to such an agreement cannot agree on an upward variation then application must be made to the C.S.A.

An applicant who is not receiving income support or income-based jobseeker's allowance can withdraw a C.S.A. application at any time or ask for an existing assessment to be cancelled.

Parents with care who are obliged to apply to the C.S.A. because they receive income support or income-based jobseeker's allowance can claim exemption from the obligation to co-operate with the maintenance assessment and to provide information to identify and trace the absent parent if there would be a risk of harm or undue distress to the applicant or a child living with the parent. The Benefits Agency cannot delay a decision on or payment of benefit if the parent claims exemption, although there is the risk of a benefits penalty being imposed. This applies where the C.S.A. is not satisfied that the parent with care has reasonable grounds for not co-operating. The penalty is currently set at a 40 per cent deduction from the parent's personal income support allowance.

The calculation

The amount of maintenance is calculated by a formula which takes into account the following:

- the maintenance requirement: this is the minimum weekly cost of caring for the child(ren) and is based on income support rates;

- exempt income: this is the income a parent can keep from his net income for his own essential expenses before child maintenance is payable. This includes housing costs and travel to work costs where the distances involved are long. A new partner's income is not included in net income;

- assessable income: this is the amount left after exempt income is deducted. Child maintenance is payable from assessable income. The basic rule is that you add together both parents' assessable incomes and take 50 per cent of the total. If that amount is less than or equal to the maintenance requirement then the maintenance payable will be 50 per cent of the absent parent's assessable income. If 50 per cent of the joint assessable income is higher than the maintenance requirement then the absent parent has to pay the whole of the maintenance requirement plus an additional payment from the remainder of his assessable income. This additional element is:

– 15 per cent where there is one qualifying child;

– 20 per cent where there are two qualifying children;

– 25 per cent where there are three or more qualifying children.

The total payable is always less than 50 per cent of the absent parent's total assessable income. There is a maximum amount of child maintenance payable under the formula. Where the maximum is being paid the parent with care can apply to court for **top-up maintenance** (see Divorce, p. 203);

- protected income: this is income which cannot be used to pay child maintenance as it is required to cover the absent parent's own needs. Basically, no absent parent has to pay more than 30 per cent of his net income as child maintenance. So if the proposed maintenance is more than that it will be reduced to 30 per cent of net income.

There are also special rules to prevent the absent parent and their second family from having their income reduced below income support level because of child maintenance payments to the first family.

Departure directions

Either the person with care or the absent parent can apply for a departure direction. This means that the C.S.A. can depart from the standard formula but only in three specific sets of circumstances:

- special expenses;
- over-generous provision;
- property or capital transfers made before April 1993.

Special expenses

You can apply for a departure direction where you:

- have travel costs in connection with exercising contact with the children named in the assessment;
- are supporting a step-child and other children in the family;
- have travel to work costs that were not taken into account in the assessment;
- or a dependant have a long-term illness or disability which involves you in additional costs;
- are paying off debts which were incurred before you and your partner separated;
- have financial commitments which were entered into pre-April 1993 and from which it would be impossible or unreasonable to withdraw.

Over-generous provision

Calculated by the formula where a parent is deliberately decreasing his available income or assets or has unreasonably high outgoings. Grounds for departure are:

- a parent's lifestyle is inconsistent with the level of his income;
- a parent's assets could produce some or more income;

- a parent has diverted his income to prevent it from being taken into account in the maintenance calculation;

- the parent's housing costs are unreasonably high;

- it is reasonable for the parent's partner to contribute towards the couple's housing costs;

- travel to work costs are unreasonably high or should be disregarded completely.

Property or capital transfers

You can get a departure direction where:

- before 5 April 1993 a court order or written agreement was in force; and

- under the order or agreement property which the absent parent owned was transferred to the person with care and **either**:

  - that transfer reduced the absent parent's maintenance liability and the effect of that transfer is not properly reflected in the current maintenance assessment; **or**

  - that transfer did not reduce the absent parent's maintenance liability but the current maintenance assessment is reduced because of that transfer and the reduction is inappropriate because of the purpose of the transfer, for example it was for spousal maintenance. This is intended to deal with situations where the absent parent transferred capital assets such as the family home to the parent with care in settlement of all financial claims including maintenance. The purpose of the departure direction is to ascertain whether the effect of that transfer is 'properly reflected' in the maintenance assessment.

Appeals

A new system of reviewing CSA decisions was introduced in 1999 with a view to simplifying the procedure. Any decision you receive from the CSA will tell you about the right of review or appeal which applies in that particular instance. It is important to observe time limits for seeking review or appeal in order to avoid losing your right.

CSA decisions are now divided into two categories:

- decisions which can be **revised, superseded** and **appealed**;
- all other decisions.

Revision

The CSA can revise a decision on any grounds if:

- the CSA starts action to revise the decision within one month of notification of the decision; or
- you apply for revision of the decision within one month of being notified of it.

Late application for revision can be allowed if there were special circumstances which prevented you from applying within the one month period but the application must have merit and it must be reasonable to grant it.

The CSA can revise a decision **at any time** if:

- your previous application for revision was refused because of insufficient evidence or information and you apply again within one month of notification of the refusal of the revision **and** provide the missing information or evidence;
- the decision arose because of 'official error', i.e. mistake by the

CSA or the Department of Social Security which was not caused or contributed to by anyone outside the CSA or the Department of Social Security;

- the decision was wrong because someone misrepresented the facts or failed to disclose material facts and benefited as a result;
- a departure direction is made with effect from the decisions effective date;
- the decision was made pending a test case decision before the courts and the courts' decision has now been given in that case.

A decision cannot be revised:

- if you have appealed against the decision and the revised decision would lead to a worse outcome for you;
- because of any change of circumstances after the effective date of the decision.

Types of decision which can be revised are:

- decision to make or refuse to make a maintenance assessment or interim maintenance assessment;
- decision to make a reduced benefit direction;
- decision to make or refuse to make a deduction of maintenance from the absent parents income support or income based jobseekers allowance;
- a decision to make or refuse to make a departure direction;
- a decision to adjust the amount of maintenance payable or to cancel an adjustment;

- any of the above decisions which have been made on supersession (see below).

Supersession

The CSA can supersede – that is, **overrule** – a decision at any time if certain requirements are met. The CSA can supersede a decision if:

- a material change in circumstances has taken place since the decision was made which will make a significant change in the amount of the maintenance assessment. Generally a significant change will be an increase or reduction in the maintenance assessment by £10.00 or more a week;
- the decision was made in ignorance of or mistake about some material fact;
- the decision is taken to make a departure direction or that decision is revised or superseded;
- the decision was made by the CSA and it is wrong in law.

The CSA cannot supersede a decision:

- which could be revised instead;
- which is a decision to make or cancel a maintenance assessment the correct procedure here is a new application.

You can apply for supersession at any time and the CSA can start supersession itself at any time.

Types of decision which can be superseded are:

- a decision to make a maintenance assessment including an interim maintenance assessment;

- a decision to make a reduced benefit direction;
- a decision to make or refuse to make a deduction of maintenance from the absent parent's income support or income based jobseekers allowance;
- a decision to make or refuse to make a departure direction;
- a decision to adjust maintenance payable or to cancel an adjustment.

Where any of the above decisions have been made on revision you can also apply for supersession of that revised decision.

Tribunal Appeals

The following CSA decisions can be appealed to an appeal tribunal:

- refusal to make a maintenance assessment or an interim maintenance assessment
- a decision to make a maintenance assessment or an interim maintenance assessment
- a decision to cancel or refuse to cancel a maintenance assessment or an interim maintenance assessment
- a decision to make a reduced benefit direction
- a decision on deduction from the absent parent's income support or income based jobseekers allowance
- a decision to make or refuse to make a departure direction.

In addition, where any of the decisions above have been made on revision or supersession you can appeal that decision. You can also appeal a refusal to revise any of the above decisions but you cannot appeal a refusal to supersede any of the above decisions.

The appeal must be made within one month of notification of the decision although extension of time for the appeal may be allowed if a good reason is advanced.

Further Appeals

The decision of the appeal tribunal can be appealed to a **Child Support Commissioner** but only on the ground of an error of law. You must get permission to appeal to the Child Support Commissioner from the appeal tribunal but if this is refused you can ask the Commissioner for permission. The refusal of permission by the Commissioner could be referred to the Court of Session under a special procedure called **judicial review** (see Glaossary). Further appeal on a point of law can be made from the Child Support Commissioner to the **Court of Session**. Again you must get permission from the Child Support Commissioner before the appeal can proceed to the Court of Session. This whole procedure is subject to time limits and qualified advice will be essential.

A detailed discussion of the Child Support Agency legislation and procedures is beyond the scope of this book. The rules and regulations are very detailed and subject to frequent alterations. Further detailed information can be obtained from the Child Support Handbook published annually by the **Child Poverty Action Group**.

Maintenance for children aged 18 or over

A child aged between 18 and 25 who is in further education or training for employment or for a trade profession or vocation can still claim aliment from their parents. The education or training must be reasonable and appropriate. No application can be made through the C.S.A. but must be made to the court. There is no formula to calculate the amount of maintenance and each case is decided on its own circumstances. The court will look at the needs, resources and earning capacities of the child and the parent.

ADOPTION

Adoption is the creation of the relationship of parent and child by court order. An adoption order gives the adoptive parents full parental responsibilities and rights in relation to the child who is treated in law as the legitimate child of the adoptive parents. The order extinguishes the parental rights and responsibilities of the child's natural parents. Adoption orders are registered in the Adopted Children's Register and the original entry of the child's birth in the Register of Births is marked 'adopted'.

There are now relatively few newborn infants put up for adoption. This reflects the facts that nowadays termination of unwanted pregnancies is generally made available and little or no stigma is attached to having a child outwith marriage. Adoption is most often used between children and step-parents and for children whose natural parents are unable or unwilling to provide them with long-term care.

Adoption agencies

Adoption must be done through an adoption agency except where the prospective adopter is a relative of the child or where a children's hearing places a child with suitable prospective adopters.

Every local authority must provide an adoption service known as an adoption agency. There are also adoption societies, which have been approved by the government to act as adoption agencies.

Criteria for adoption

The court and the adoption agency must look at all the circumstances of the case in reaching any decision in relation to adopting a child. The paramount consideration is the need to safeguard and promote the child's welfare throughout their life. They must also have regard to the child's views if they want to express them, taking into account their age and maturity, and to their religion, racial origin and cultural and linguistic background. Adoption agencies must also consider the natural parents' wishes regarding the child's religious upbringing.

Who can be adopted?

Children who are under 18 and are not and have not been married. A child aged 12 or over must give their consent to the adoption order otherwise it cannot be made.

Who can adopt?

- an unmarried person aged 21 or over;
- a married couple both aged 21 or over can adopt jointly;
- a married person can adopt alone if their spouse cannot be found or cannot make a joint application because of physical or mental ill health or the spouses are permanently separated;
- a step-parent who is married to the natural parent of the child.

Procedure

The application for an adoption order is made to the Court of Session or the sheriff court in the area where the child lives. The court must appoint a *curator ad litem* (usually a solicitor who is not otherwise involved in the case) whose duty it is to safeguard the child's interests. The *curator ad litem* must provide the court with a full report dealing with all the circumstances of the adoption application, to give the court an independent view of whether adoption is in the child's best interests.

Parental agreement

An adoption order cannot be made unless the court is satisfied that each parent or guardian of the child consents to the order freely and with full understanding of what is involved. 'Parent' means mother and father who both have parental rights and responsibilities. Where only one has parental rights and responsibilities only that parent's consent is required. Therefore an unmarried father who has not acquired parental rights and responsibilities is not a parent for this purpose. Any other individual who has acquired parental rights and responsibilities is not treated as a parent for this purpose either and their consent is not required.

Freeing a child for adoption

A freeing order is an order obtained by an adoption agency, which is a local authority, transferring parental rights and responsibilities for the child from the child's parent or guardian to the adoption agency to enable it to proceed with the adoption. This must be made with the consent of the parent or guardian unless the child is already being looked after by the adoption agency, in which case the parent or guardian's consent to the freeing order is not required as long as the agency is applying to the court to dispense with the agreement of the parent or guardian to the adoption.

Where a freeing order has been granted the parent or guardian is entitled after a year to be told by the agency whether the child has been adopted or placed for adoption. If the child has not been adopted or placed for adoption the parent or guardian may apply to the court to cancel the freeing order and try to regain their parental responsibilities and rights.

Dispensation with parental agreement

Where a child is not freed for adoption the parent or guardian must agree to the adoption order otherwise it cannot be made. The court does, however, have the power to dispense with the parent or guardian's agreement to the adoption order or their consent to a freeing order if the parent or guardian:

- is not known, cannot be found or is incapable of giving agreement;

- is withholding agreement unreasonably;

- has persistently failed without reasonable cause to safeguard and promote the child's health, development and welfare or if the child is not living with them has persistently failed to maintain regular contact with the child;

- has seriously ill-treated the child and the child is unlikely, because of that ill-treatment, to go back and live with the parent.

To dispense with parental agreement the court must:

- establish that one of the above grounds exists; and

- consider whether consent should be dispensed with on that ground.

The second ground (agreement being withheld unreasonably) is the one that most commonly results in court proceedings. The court must consider all the circumstances of the case and ask itself what a 'reasonable' parent would do in the circumstances.

Parents who consider that they do have good reason for withholding their agreement to an adoption order being made should always seek legal advice.

Re-establishing contact between the adopted child and the natural parents

Once the adopted child is 16 he can have access to his original birth certificate to establish his natural parentage. Adoption agencies must provide counselling for those whose adoptions they arranged where they are seeking information about their natural parents.

PROTECTION OF CHILDREN IN NEED

It is accepted in our society that parents and families should be left to make their own arrangements for the care and upbringing of children. However it is also recognised that there will be situations where parents are unable or unwilling to make such arrangements. To protect children in that situation the law imposes a duty on local authorities:

- to give general advice, guidance and assistance to those living in its area;

- to safeguard and promote the welfare of children in need in its area; and

- in fulfilment of that duty, to promote the upbringing of such children by their families and to help the children within their home environment.

The emphasis is very much on flexible solutions with the aim of supporting the family unit as a whole and enabling the child to remain there if at all possible rather than the local authority taking over the role of the parent. This can, of course, still happen in extreme situations. Parents or others with parental rights and responsibilities can voluntarily place a child in local authority care (for example, where a parent is ill and unable to look after the child). The local authority can arrange to place the child with relatives, foster carers or in local authority accommodation. In accommodating the child the local authority is under a duty to:

- take account of the child's views, having regard to their age and maturity;

- ascertain the parents' wishes and the wishes of any other relevant person;

- take account of the child's age and understanding, religion, racial origins and cultural and linguistic background.

The parent or other person with parental rights and responsibilities who has placed the child in local authority care retains their parental rights and responsibilities and can remove the child from local authority care at any time, unless the child has been in care for a continuous period of six months or more when at least 14 days' notice of removal must be given.

Orders a local authority can obtain

Child assessment order

If a child's family denies access to the child (the child for this purpose being under the age of 16) and the social work department requires access in order to assess the child's needs it can apply to the sheriff court for a child assessment order to enable it to assess the state of the child's health or development or the way in which the child has been treated. Before granting the order the sheriff must be satisfied that:

- the local authority has reasonable grounds for suspecting that the child is suffering or likely to suffer significant harm; and
- the assessment is needed to establish whether or not there is reasonable cause to believe the child is being badly treated or neglected; and
- it is unlikely that such an assessment will be made in the absence of a court order.

Exclusion order

This order was introduced by the Children (Scotland) Act 1995 to deal with the situation where a child under the age of 16 is being abused at home. Previously, a child in that situation would have to be removed from the home for their own protection. The new law allows the local authority to apply to the court for an order excluding the abuser from the child's family home instead. The sheriff may grant the order if:

- the child is suffering or is likely to suffer significant harm because of the behaviour or threatened or feared behaviour of the abuser; and

- the making of the exclusion order is necessary for the protection of the child and would better safeguard the child's welfare than removal of the child from the family home; and

- if the order is made there will be someone in the home (who must be named in the order) who is capable of taking responsibility for caring for the child and any member of the family who requires care.

An exclusion order lasts for six months and cannot be renewed.

Parental responsibilities order

The local authority can obtain a parental responsibilities order to transfer parental responsibilities and rights from the parents or other person having parental responsibilities and rights to the local authority in respect of a child under the age of 18. This order cannot be made unless the person with parental responsibilities and rights:

- agrees to the order freely and with full understanding of what is involved; or

- is a person who:
  - is not known, cannot be found or is incapable of giving agreement;
  - is withholding agreement unreasonably;
  - has persistently failed without reasonable cause to safeguard and promote the child's health, development and welfare or if the child is not living with him has persistently failed to maintain regular contact with the child;

– has seriously ill-treated the child and the child is unlikely, because of that ill-treatment, to go back and live with the parents.

In granting any of the above orders the court must always regard the child's welfare as the paramount consideration. It must also be satisfied that making an order would be better for the child than not making one and it must take account of the child's views where appropriate.

THE CHILDREN'S PANEL

This replaced the former court-based juvenile criminal justice system and also created a scheme to provide **compulsory measures of care** necessary where it is not possible to provide appropriate support for the child under the local authority's powers referred to above. Compulsory measures of care and **supervision** (see p. 198) are made by a children's hearing. As usual the paramount consideration is the welfare of the child throughout their childhood, although the children's hearing can depart from that principle in order to protect the public from serious harm.

A child can only be referred to a children's hearing by a reporter to the Childrens Panel. This happens when the reporter receives information that a child may need compulsory measures of care or supervision. This information can come from a local authority, the police, the courts or even members of the public. The reporter must investigate the matter and then decide:

• to take no further action; or
• to refer the case to the local authority for the family to receive social work support; or

- if the reporter considers that the child is in need of compulsory measures of supervision, to arrange a children's hearing and ask the local authority for a report on the child and their social background.

Three members of the Children's Panel, who are people with a knowledge of or interest in children, conduct the children's hearing. The reporter is present during the hearing, as are the child and any relevant person.

A relevant person is:

- any parent with parental rights and responsibilities;
- any person who has been awarded parental rights and responsibilities by the court (for example, a grandparent who has a residence order);
- any person who appears ordinarily to have charge of or control over the child (for example, an unmarried father who does not have parental rights and responsibilities but who lives with the child).

What are the grounds of referral to a children's hearing?

Briefly, these are that:

- the child is beyond the control of any relevant person; or
- the child is falling into bad company or moral danger; or
- lack of parental care is likely to cause the child unnecessary suffering or seriously affect the child's health or development; or
- the child is a victim of a criminal offence listed in Schedule 1

to the Criminal Procedure (Scotland) Act 1995. These offences include physical or sexual assault and incest;

- the child is or is likely to become a member of the same household as a child who has been the victim of a criminal offence;

- the child is or is likely to become a member of the same household as a person who has committed a criminal offence listed in Schedule 1 to the Criminal Procedure (Scotland) Act 1995. (N.B. The offence does not have to have been committed against the child in question);

- the child is or is likely to become a member of the same household as a person who has been the victim of incest or intercourse with a step-parent or person in a position of trust committed by a member of that household; or

- the child has failed to attend school regularly without reasonable excuse; or

- the child has committed a crime. Where the child has committed very serious crimes such as murder or rape or has committed an offence along with an adult the child can be prosecuted in the criminal courts instead. The child must be aged eight or over to be referred to the Panel under this ground or to be prosecuted in the criminal courts;

- the child has misused drugs or alcohol; or

- the child has been glue sniffing; or

- the child is in local authority care or is the subject of a parental responsibilities order and his behaviour is such that special measures of supervision are necessary in the child's own interests or in the interests of others.

Disposal of the case

The children's hearing must explain the grounds of referral to the child and the relevant person. If they accept the grounds of referral the hearing then decides how to dispose of the case.

Refusal to accept the grounds of referral

If the child or relevant person does not accept or understand the grounds of referral the children's hearing must either discharge the referral or direct the reporter to apply to the sheriff court to decide whether or not the grounds of referral are established. The court hearing must be held within 28 days of the application being lodged in court. The child has the right to be present at the court hearing. The child and the relevant person(s) have the right to be represented in court. The representative can be a lawyer and legal aid is available for both the child and the relevant person. The reporter must bring evidence to establish that the grounds of referral exist. If the sheriff is satisfied by the evidence that some or all of the grounds do exist, the case goes back to the children's hearing for disposal. If the sheriff is satisfied that none of the grounds of referral is established the case is dismissed and the referral is discharged.

Once the grounds of referral have been accepted by the child and the relevant person or held to have been established by the sheriff the hearing then decides how to dispose of the case. In doing so it can make one of three disposals:

- to continue the case to another hearing, if it considers that further investigation is needed before it can make a decision. It can grant a warrant to put the child in a place of safety for up to 22 days until the court hearing. This may be done where it is necessary to safeguard or promote a child's welfare or if there is reason to believe that the child will not attend the continued hearing;

- discharge the referral, if no further action is needed;

- make a supervision requirement. This can include any condition which will safeguard and promote the child's welfare. This is a very wide-ranging power and it is not possible to list all the conditions which a supervision requirement might contain, as each case will depend on its own facts. Some of the most common examples of conditions in supervision requirements are, however:

  – to require the child to live at any place specified in the requirement, for example local authority accommodation or a relative's home;

  – to require a child to submit to medical examination or other treatment

    N.B. the child can still refuse to consent to such examination or treatment if he has capacity (see p. 162);

  – to require a child not to have contact with an individual named in the supervision requirement (for example, where an individual is suspected of physically or sexually abusing a child).

Where the supervision requirement provides that a child is not to live with his family it can make a condition that there should be contact between the child and any other person.

The children's hearing must ask for the child's views about the supervision requirement. As usual, the child is not obliged to give a view and even if he does the hearing is not obliged to give effect to that view (for example, where the child's views are not consistent with what is in their interests). The **minimum intervention principle** applies in that the hearing must be satisfied that it is better for the child for it to make the supervision requirement than for it to make no supervision requirement at all.

The supervision requirement should only continue for as long as it is in the child's interests. It cannot continue beyond the child's 18th birthday. A supervision requirement can only last for a year unless it has been continued within the year at a review by the children's hearing.

The child or any relevant person can ask for a review of the supervision requirement at any time after it has been in place for three months. The children's hearing itself can fix a review date at the time when it makes its original disposal. The local authority can ask for a review at any time.

The supervision requirement does not deprive the parents of their parental rights and responsibilities but it does restrict their operation. For example if the supervision requirement requires the child to live in local authority care the parent cannot exercise the right to decide where the child shall live. Similarly, a parent could obtain a court order for contact while the child is subject to a supervision requirement but if the supervision requirement says that the child is not to have contact with that parent they cannot exercise the order.

Appeal against the decision of the children's hearing

A child or the relevant person has the right of appeal to the sheriff court if they disagree with the decision of the children's hearing. If the court is satisfied that the decision of the hearing is not justi-fied in all the circumstances of the case it can make one of three disposals:

- send the case back to the children's hearing to re-consider its decision;
- discharge the referral;
- substitute its own decision for that of the hearing.

Emergency protection for children and child protection orders

A child protection order is the emergency procedure for bringing a child before the children's hearing. Any person (but in practice usually a local authority) can apply to the sheriff court for a child protection order. The court may make such an order if it is satis-fied that:

- there are reasonable grounds to believe that the child is suffer-ing significant harm because of the way they are being treated or neglected; or
- the child will suffer significant harm if not removed to and kept in a place of safety; and
- a child protection order is necessary to protect the child from significant harm. If a local authority has applied for an assess-ment order (see p. 192) but the court considers that the con-ditions for a child protection order are satisfied in the appli-cation it must grant a child protection order. The court can also order or prohibit parental contact with the child while the child is in a place of safety.

There must be a children's hearing on the second working day after the child protection order has been implemented, to decide whether the child protection order should continue. If the children's hearing is satisfied that the child protection order was necessary it can continue the order to a second hearing to decide whether the child is in need of compulsory measures of supervision (see p. 00). The second hearing must take place on the eighth working day after the child protection order has been implemented.

There is no appeal against the court's decision to grant a child protection order or against the first children's hearing's decision to continue the order. You can, however, apply to the court to have the child protection order recalled or varied. This application must be made before the first children's hearing is heard. Similarly, you can ask the court to recall or vary the decision of the first children's hearing but this must be done within two working days of the decision.

If the case cannot be disposed of at the second children's hearing the Panel can issue a warrant to keep the child in the place of safety up to a maximum of 66 days from the date when the child was first taken to a place of safety.

When does a child protection order cease to have effect?

- if no attempt has been made to implement it by 24 hours after it was made;

- where the first children's hearing does not continue the child protection order;

- where an application to recall the child protection order is not decided within three days of it being made;

- where the court recalls the order;
- where the reporter considers that the order is no longer appropriate;
- where the second children's hearing has commenced.

8 Divorce

Divorce on the grounds of adultery and desertion has been part of Scots law for hundreds of years. Further grounds of divorce – cruelty, incurable insanity, sodomy and bestiality – were introduced in the 1930s. Divorce law was based on the concept of there being a 'guilty party' and an 'innocent party', with only the 'innocent' spouse being able to seek a divorce.

By the 1960s it was recognised that it was not in the public interest to try to keep alive marriages which were over and that the concepts of 'guilt' and 'innocence' in relation to marital breakdown were no longer necessarily appropriate in every situation. It was proposed that **irretrievable breakdown of marriage** should be the sole ground of divorce. This reform was introduced by the Divorce (Scotland) Act 1976. It was considered, however, that some definition of what constituted irretrievable breakdown would be required. This led to it being established in law by evidence of one of the following five factors:

- adultery;
- unreasonable behaviour by one party;
- desertion;

- two years' separation of the parties, with the consent of the party not bringing the divorce action;
- five years' separation of the parties, irrespective of whether the party not bringing the action consents.

Britain has the highest divorce rate in Europe, with more than 40 per cent of marriages ending in divorce. The Scottish Parliament is currently considering further reform of divorce law by reducing the time periods for the separation factors to one year and two years respectively.

SEEKING A DIVORCE

Jurisdiction

A divorcing couple must first establish whether the Scottish courts have jurisdiction to hear their case. In other words, can they get divorced in Scotland?

The majority of divorces in Scotland proceed in the sheriff court. A divorce case can proceed in the sheriff court only if either party to the marriage:

- is domiciled in Scotland at the date when the action is begun; or
- was habitually resident there throughout the period of one year ending with the date when the action was begun;

and

- either party to the marriage was resident in the particular sheriff court district for a period of 40 days ending with that date; or

- if no longer residing in Scotland, did reside for at least 40 days in the sheriff court district, that period ending no later than 40 days before the action is raised.

The Court of Session has jurisdiction to hear an action of divorce if either of the first two grounds above is satisfied. Generally, actions are raised in the Court of Session only where the parties are wealthy, with complex financial affairs, or where there are matters of international law affecting the welfare of children of the marriage.

If irretrievable breakdown is established, divorce proceedings can be raised at any time after the date of the marriage. (Compare the position in England, where a year must elapse between the date of the marriage and the date of divorce proceedings.)

Domicile and habitual residence

A discussion of the concept of domicile is beyond the scope and purpose of this book. In general terms, if you are domiciled in Scotland it means that you regard Scotland as your home. This does not necessarily mean that you have to live here full-time. For example, if you were born in Scotland but spent much of your adult life working and living abroad you can still claim Scottish domicile.

The concept of habitual residence is more readily understandable. It is a question of the fact of where a person usually lives. Short absences abroad for work or holidays do not count against the one-year period required to establish habitual residence.

When can the court refuse to hear divorce proceedings because of jurisdiction issues?

You must advise the court if you know of ongoing proceedings in any other country which could affect your marriage.

If those other proceedings are **within the U.K.** and the following conditions are satisfied then the Scottish courts **must**, if asked to do so, sist (i.e suspend) the Scottish action. The conditions are that:

- the couple must have lived together after the date of the marriage;
- the place where they lived together when the Scottish action was begun (or if they were not living together then the place where they last lived together before that date) is in another part of the U.K.;
- either of them normally lived in that other part of the U.K. throughout the year ending with the date of their separation before the Scottish action was begun.

If the other proceedings are **outwith the U.K.** the Scottish court may be asked to sist (suspend) the Scottish action but does not **have** to do so. The Scottish action can be sisted if it appears to the court that the balance of fairness (including convenience) as between the parties to the marriage is such that it is appropriate for the foreign proceedings to be disposed of before further steps are taken in the Scottish action.

Factors which the court can consider are where the matrimonial property is situated, where the parties to the marriage reside and where most of the witnesses who will be required in the divorce action are based.

ESTABLISHING IRRETRIEVABLE BREAKDOWN

Irretrievable breakdown is the **only** ground for divorce. This is established by evidence of one of the five factors mentioned at the beginning of the chapter.

The spouse who asks for the divorce is called the **pursuer**; the other spouse is the **defender**.

Adultery

Irretrievable breakdown is established if, since the date of the marriage, the defender has committed adultery. Adultery is **voluntary** sexual intercourse between a married person and **a person of the opposite sex** who is not the marriage partner. A woman who has been raped cannot be guilty of adultery. The sexual act must be heterosexual and so a gay or lesbian sexual act cannot constitute adultery although it could give rise to a divorce on the basis of the defender's unreasonable behaviour. The parties to the marriage do not need to have been living together when the adultery took place.

Adultery can be proved by an admission from the defender and the person with whom he has committed adultery (known as the paramour). The paramour must be named in the divorce action and must have notice of the action served on them. Where the defender and paramour refuse to co-operate in providing admissions (and they cannot be forced to do so) the other most common way to obtain the necessary evidence is for private investigators to be instructed to carry out covert observations of the defender and the paramour. For a divorce to be granted on the basis of adultery there must always be evidence from a third party. In other words, the evidence of the pursuer and the defender alone are not sufficient.

There are two possible defences to adultery, apart from the

obvious one that it did not in fact take place. Neither of these defences is very common nowadays.

The first is that where a pursuer actively **promoted** or arranged for the defender to commit adultery, the pursuer cannot found on that adultery in order to raise divorce proceedings. Therefore a man who puts his wife out to prostitution cannot rely on that to raise divorce proceedings based on adultery.

The second defence is that the defender's adultery has been **condoned**, or accepted, by the pursuer continuing to live with the defender in the knowledge or belief that he or she has committed adultery. The basic rule is that the adultery is only condoned if the pursuer lives with the defender for a period of more than three months after the pursuer knows or believes the defender to have committed adultery.

Unreasonable behaviour

Irretrievable breakdown is established if, since the date of the marriage, the defender has at any time behaved in such a way that the pursuer cannot reasonably be expected to cohabit with the defender.

It does not matter that the behaviour occurs as a result of mental abnormality over which the defender has no control. The behaviour can be active or passive. It must occur **after** the date of the marriage. What the court must look at is whether, at the time the action goes to court, the pursuer can reasonably be expected to cohabit with the defender. The test is both objective and subjective. This is in recognition of the fact that while utterly trivial conduct should not be allowed to constitute grounds for divorce, different people have different tolerance levels and what one person might consider acceptable conduct another might find intolerable. In essence each case turns on its own facts and circumstances. The commonest types of behaviour giving rise to 'unreasonable behaviour' divorces are:

- alcohol abuse;
- drug abuse;
- violence or attempted or threatened violence towards the pursuer and/or the children of the marriage;
- gay or lesbian relationships; and
- incest.

These are only examples and many types of behaviour falling outwith this list have been held to establish irretrievable breakdown under this ground.

The conduct can take place on a regular basis or be a build-up of isolated incidents. In rare cases, a single incident can be so destructive of the marital relationship that it can constitute grounds for divorce even if there is no risk of the conduct being repeated.

The fact that a pursuer continues to live with the defender after the behaviour took place is not in itself a bar to founding on the behaviour for the purposes of divorce.

Where a 'behaviour' divorce is undefended the pursuer must still prove the allegations he or she makes, on a balance of probabilities, and the court will not simply 'rubber stamp' the divorce action. At the same time, however, it will not conduct lengthy enquiries into behaviour where one spouse has declared that the marriage is at an end.

Desertion

Irretrievable breakdown is established if the defender has, wilfully and without reasonable cause, deserted the pursuer and during a continuous period of two years immediately after the desertion the parties have not cohabited and the pursuer has not refused a genuine and reasonable offer by the defender to live together.

The desertion must be wilful – in other words, the defender must intend to leave and end the marriage. It therefore follows that the defender's detention in prison, absence on overseas posting or a long-term stay in hospital cannot establish desertion.

The pursuer must be willing for the parties to live together when the defender leaves. Therefore, if the parties agree to separate there is no desertion.

The parties must cease to cohabit as man and wife. This can be established even if they continue to live under the same roof.

The defender must leave without reasonable cause. So, if the defender leaves because of the pursuer's adultery or unreasonable behaviour, that is not desertion, provided that these reasons existed at the time of departure.

There must be two years' continuous non-cohabitation and during that time the pursuer must not refuse a genuine and reasonable offer from the defender for the parties to live together.

Desertion is a factor which is rarely relied on nowadays.

Two years' separation with consent

Irretrievable breakdown is established if there has been no cohabitation between the parties at any time during a continuous period of two years after the date of the marriage and immediately preceding the bringing of the action, and the defender consents to the divorce.

Cohabitation

'Cohabitation' in this context means living together as husband and wife. The reason why the parties are not living together does not matter here – the mere fact of physical separation is sufficient. This is logical, as the basis for the action is mutual consent. Two years' separation can be established even where the couple continue to live under the same roof, as long as they can show that they were not living together as husband and wife (i.e. no sexual relationship, separate bedrooms, separate domestic arrangements, separate social lives).

The separation must be for a **continuous** period of two years. If the parties lived together again as husband and wife for a period of six months or less during the separation, and then separate again, the period of non-cohabitation still runs from the original date of separation but the period for which they lived together again does not count towards the two years.

Consent must be given in the proper form. The defender must be served with the divorce papers, which will include a prescribed consent form and information sheet about the consequences of consenting to divorce. The defender must sign and return the form to the court. If it is not returned the divorce cannot proceed. The defender can withdraw his or her consent at any time and for any reason or no reason at all. The defender must write to the court intimating withdrawal of consent.

Five years' separation

Irretrievable breakdown is established if there has been no cohabitation between the parties at any time during a continuous period of five years after the date of the marriage and immediately preceding the bringing of the divorce action.

The definition of 'cohabitation' and the continuity of the period of separation are the same as in two-year separation cases. The court is not bound to grant the divorce if in its opinion the divorce would result in grave financial hardship to the defender.

JUDICIAL SEPARATION

The factors justifying a judicial separation are identical to the five factors establishing the ground for divorce. The court orders the parties to live apart but does not end the marriage. This is used when parties have a religious or other objection to the concept of divorce. The spouses continue to have an obligation to aliment (maintain) each other but the court in a judicial separation has no power to divide up matrimonial assets.

Judicial separations are not common nowadays and the Scottish Law Commission has recommended its abolition.

SEEKING AN AMICABLE PARTING

Reconciliation

As a matter of public policy, the law provides that if at any time before divorce is granted it appears to the court that there is a reasonable prospect of reconciliation between the spouses a divorce action can be suspended to allow an attempt at reconciliation to take place. If parties are reconciled but the reconciliation then fails the reconciliation period does not affect the divorce proceedings, which can then carry on. In practice, this provision is rarely used.

Mediation

Reconciliation is an attempt by the parties to live together again as husband and wife. Mediation, on the other hand, is intended to assist in making their parting as amicable as possible. There are two types of mediation:

- mediation on matters involving parental rights and responsibilities. Parties can attend this type of mediation voluntarily, either before or after court proceedings have been raised. In addition, the court also has the power to refer parties to this type of mediation in any family action dealing with parental rights and responsibilities. These mediation services are operated locally throughout Scotland under the auspices of Family Mediation Scotland. It charges no fee for its services. It attempts to narrow the areas of dispute between the parties and assist them in reaching agreement on matters such as with which parent children should live and arrangements for contact with the other parent;

- mediation covering all aspects of marital breakdown, including financial aspects. The Law Society of Scotland operates a mediation service called CALM whose mediators are qualified solicitors. A fee is payable for its services but this cost may be covered by legal aid, depending on your financial circumstances. Both parties attend mediation sessions with the aim of drawing up a comprehensive agreement dealing with all aspects of their separation. It is recommended that once this agreement is reached each party takes independent advice on its terms from his or her own solicitor before the agreement is finalised.

The final agreement has to be drawn up by the parties' solicitors, not by the mediator.

The same result can be, and often is, achieved by negotiation between parties' solicitors without the involvement of a mediator. This can happen where parties have agreed to go their separate ways and wish to negotiate a settlement on matters such as care arrangements for children, maintenance and division of property. Each party should provide a full and frank disclosure of income and assets and agreement is then negotiated on matters such as:

- where the children will live and their contact with the other parent;
- payment of spousal maintenance and child maintenance;
- payment of school fees;
- occupation or sale of the matrimonial home; and
- division of other property.

These are just some of the matters which can be dealt with in a separation agreement but the couple can include whatever other matters are relevant to them. The separation agreement is a binding and enforceable contract resolving all matters so that the divorce action itself need not deal with them but is simply the final step in dissolving the legal bond of marriage.

The court does have power to alter the terms of a separation agreement regarding the welfare of children but can only interfere with agreed financial arrangements in the following circumstances:

- where the agreement says that the court can alter the amount of maintenance for a spouse; or

- where the agreement was not fair and reasonable at the time it was entered into.

DIVORCE PROCEDURE

D.I.Y. or 'quickie' divorces

These terms are often used in the mistaken belief that there is some other special swift divorce procedure available to parties who are in agreement that their marriage should be ended. This is not so. The only ground for divorce is irretrievable breakdown on the basis of the five factors outlined on page 203.

In theory, anyone can appear as a party litigant (i.e. without a solicitor) in a Scottish divorce action. In practice, however, it is advisable to seek help from a solicitor. Divorce law can be complex and the papers which have to be submitted to the court must follow a certain format. The divorce action itself follows certain procedural rules.

However, a form of D.I.Y. divorce is available in certain limited circumstances. This is called the **simplified procedure** and requires the parties to have been separated for two or five years. There must be no children of the marriage under the age of 16 years and neither party can seek financial provision on divorce (see p. 220). The appropriate forms can be obtained from the sheriff clerk's office of the local sheriff court and the staff there will also provide guidance regarding completion of the form and payment of the court fee, etc.

Other divorces, defended and undefended

All other divorce actions in the sheriff court are commenced by lodging a document known as an **initial writ**. Unlike in England, where there are standard forms which are simply filled in, in Scotland the initial writ must be drawn up from scratch. It must state the legal remedies the pursuer seeks, for example divorce, orders in relation to children and orders for financial provision, and the facts upon which these remedies are sought.

Once the writ is drafted, it is sent to the sheriff clerk's office together with the parties' marriage certificate and the birth certificates of any children of the marriage under the age of 16. The sheriff clerk grants warrant to serve the initial writ on the defender. Service can also be ordered on other parties who have an interest in the action. The defender then has 21 days from the date of service to advise the court if they will defend the action. This is done by returning a notice of intention to defend which the defender receives along with the writ.

Defended actions

If the defender intends to **defend** the action they must lodge defences stating the basis of their opposition. The defences can also include legal remedies sought by the defender (called a counterclaim) in relation to the children or financial provision.

The action then proceeds in accordance with the Sheriff Court Rules applicable to family actions. Even though an action starts out as defended, parties may negotiate a settlement of the defended aspects at any time up to the point when the case comes to proof and the action can then proceed as undefended (see Undefended actions, p. 217). If no agreement is reached then there must be a proof. This is a hearing at which parties and their witnesses give evidence before the sheriff who then decides how to dispose of the case.

Undefended actions

If no notice of intention to defend is lodged the divorce can proceed as **undefended**, with proof by affidavits. This means that the pursuer's evidence and that of any witnesses is given by way of a written statement sworn before a solicitor, rather than by going into court and giving evidence from the witness box. Once the court is satisfied that on the basis of the evidence divorce can be allowed, it grants the decree of divorce together with any other orders which have been sought. A period of 14 days must elapse between the granting of decree and the issuing of the extract, which is the document which proves that the parties are divorced.

LEGAL AID

Legal aid is available in connection with matters arising from separation and divorce, provided that you fulfil the financial eligibility requirements. Legal aid is available in connection with actual court proceedings, including undefended divorces. A limited form of legal aid, called 'legal advice and assistance', is available to cover receiving advice on and drawing up separation agreements and arranging comprehensive family mediation.

CHILDREN

The law imposes certain limited restrictions on the granting of divorce where the parties have children under the age of 16. The court must consider, in the light of such information as it has before it about the arrangements for the upbringing of the children, whether it should make any order in relation to the children. The court can make the following orders:

- a residence order;

- a contact order;

- an order depriving parents of some or all parental rights and/or responsibilities;

- a specific issue order;

- an interdict;

- an order regarding management of a child's property.

- An order referring a child to a Children's Panel (see Children, p. 153)

If the court decides that it has to do any of the above but cannot do so without giving further consideration to the case, and there are exceptional circumstances which make it desirable in the interests of the child that the divorce should not be granted until one of the above orders has been made, then it can postpone the granting of the divorce.

Essentially, however, the court can only postpone granting decree of divorce in exceptional circumstances which relate to the welfare of the child.

CHILD MAINTENANCE ON DIVORCE

Both parents continue to have an obligation to maintain their children on divorce. The Child Support Act 1991 deprived the courts of their jurisdiction to deal with child maintenance except in certain limited circumstances. On separation or divorce either the parent with whom the children continue to live (called the

parent with care) or the other parent (called the **absent parent**) can apply to the Child Support Agency (C.S.A.) for a maintenance assessment. This is the C.S.A.'s assessment of how much child maintenance the absent parent should pay. Maintenance assessments can only be made for the couple's own children, or their adopted children. The parent with care cannot get a maintenance assessment for children who are the step-children of the absent parent. For example, a woman marries her second husband and they live together with her children from her first marriage whom he accepts as children of the family. When the marriage breaks down, if the children remain with the mother she cannot get a maintenance assessment order for the children because they are not her husband's children but only his step-children. She would have to apply to the **court** for a maintenance order.

The court can also make orders for maintenance for a couple's own or adopted children, **in addition** to the C.S.A. maintenance assessment, in the following circumstances:

- where the absent parent is wealthy enough to pay more maintenance than the maximum award allowable under the C.S.A. formula. This is commonly known as a **top-up award**;

- to cover payment of school fees or fees in connection with training for a trade, profession or vocation;

- to cover some or all of the expenses of a disabled child, which expenses arise out of the child's disability.

Where the parent with care is in receipt of income support or income-based jobseeker's allowance assessment of child maintenance by the C.S.A. is **compulsory**. In all other situations parents can **agree** the issue of child maintenance in a written minute of agreement **without** involving the C.S.A. It is intended that eventually the C.S.A. will regulate all child maintenance payments and so in due course such agreements will be overturned by the C.S.A. but in practical terms it is likely to be several more years before that is achieved. In the meantime, therefore, if you believe that you would be better off in relation to child maintenance under a written agreement rather than under a C.S.A. assessment you should try to negotiate such an agreement. The existence of such an agreement then prevents application to the C.S.A. unless the parent with care then starts to receive any of the benefits or allowances just mentioned, in which case the C.S.A. can overturn the agreement.

FINANCIAL PROVISION FOR SPOUSES ON DIVORCE

On the breakdown of a marriage it is important that each spouse should seek independent legal advice on how to protect their interests and to inform them of the nature and extent of their rights and obligations in relation to financial matters. Spouses should not be put off consulting their solicitors at the earliest opportunity for fear of incurring large legal bills. Most matrimonial lawyers will provide a free brief initial interview at which eligibility for legal aid and hourly rates for private work can be discussed. Consulting a solicitor does not mean that you are immediately obliged to go to court to litigate over who gets what. Indeed most family law practitioners will advise against immediate court action unless it is absolutely necessary, preferring to encourage their clients to try to reach an amicable settlement.

MATRIMONIAL PROPERTY

How is this defined?

It is all the property belonging to the parties or to either of them **at the relevant date**, which was acquired by them or either of them during the marriage but before the relevant date. A house acquired before the marriage for use by the parties as a family home, and the household contents, are also defined as matrimonial property. Gifts from one spouse to another are matrimonial property but gifts to them or either of them by third parties are not. Similarly, money or other items inherited from a third party are not matrimonial property.

Matrimonial property can therefore include the family home, contents, savings, family cars, life insurance policies and rights under a pension scheme. Property owned by either spouse **before** the marriage (with the exception of the family home, outlined above) is **not** matrimonial property although the court can take this into account as a resource of the spouse who owns it, in assessing how the matrimonial property should be divided.

Relevant date

This is **either**:

- the date on which the parties ceased to cohabit; or
- the date of service of the divorce summons, whichever occurs **first**.

This is the date at which the value of the matrimonial property is established. It is of considerable significance, particularly in relation to assets which may fluctuate or dramatically increase or decrease in value.

Net value of the matrimonial property

This is the value of the property at the relevant date after deductions of any debts incurred by the parties or either of them before the marriage if they relate to the matrimonial property and during the marriage which are outstanding at the relevant date.

The basic principles

The basic principles which the court must apply in dividing up the matrimonial property are that:

- **the net value of the matrimonial property should be shared fairly between the parties to the marriage.** 'Fair' sharing is defined as equal sharing unless there are special circumstances (see p. 224);

- **fair account should be taken of any economic advantage derived by either party from contributions by the other and of any economic disadvantage suffered by either party in the interests of the other party or the family.** An example of this would be where a wife gave up a well-paid career to have and look after children or to assist her husband in his chosen career. 'Contribution' means a contribution made whether before or during the marriage and includes indirect and non-financial contributions. Looking after the family home and caring for the family are specifically recognised;

- **the economic burden of caring after divorce for a child of the marriage under the age of 16 years should be shared**

fairly between the parties. This principle recognises that payment of maintenance alone for a child may not be sufficient to ensure fair sharing of the burden of childcare. The parent who has the children may have to give up work, work part-time or pay for childcare. They will have to maintain a home for the children and bear the costs that go with it. This principle can be used to justify an award of more than half the matrimonial property to the parent with care of the children if the court accepts that that is necessary to distribute the burden of child-care fairly. A parent with care can also be awarded **periodical allowance** (see p. 227);

- **a party who has been dependent to a substantial degree on the financial support of the other party should be awarded such financial provision as is reasonable to enable them to adjust over a period of not more than three years from the date of the divorce to the loss of financial support on divorce.** The intention here is to provide financial support for a spouse, usually a wife, to enable them to adjust to becoming self-supporting again. If a wife has continued to work full-time during the marriage or has found full-time employment between the dates of separation and divorce this provision may not apply. It can be used where a spouse is undertaking further education or re-training following separation and divorce. The financial provision can be in the form of a **lump sum payment** or **property transfer order** or, if either of these is not sufficient, weekly or monthly payment of **periodical allowance** can be awarded, but only for a maximum period of three years (see p. 227);

- **a party who at the time of divorce seems likely to suffer serious financial hardship as a result of the divorce should be awarded such financial provision as is reasonable to relieve them of the hardship over a reasonable period.** This can be done by awarding a **property transfer order** and/or a **capital sum** and/or **periodical allowance** (see p.227). The purpose of this principle is to cover those situations where application of the previous four principles would not provide adequate financial provision. This will usually be where, at the time of the divorce, the applicant is elderly or infirm and unable to work and because of that will suffer serious financial hardship.

Special circumstances

These can include:

- the terms of any agreement between the parties on the ownership or division of any of the matrimonial property;

- the source of money or assets used to acquire matrimonial property where the money or assets did not come from the income or efforts of the parties during the marriage;

- destruction or squandering or giving away property by either party;

- the nature of the matrimonial property, the use made of it (including use for business purposes or matrimonial home) and the extent to which it is reasonable to expect it to be sold or divided or used as security;

- actual or future liability for the expenses of valuation or transfer of property in connection with the divorce.

Special circumstances are not limited to those listed above. The usefulness of a special circumstance argument has been limited by the courts' interpretation of the application of this section. The current position is that simply because special circumstances exist the court is not obliged to make an unequal division of matrimonial property. The court must first be satisfied that special circumstances do exist and thereafter be satisfied that their existence **justifies** an unequal division of the net value of the matrimonial property.

A 'clean break'

The thinking behind the modern law on financial provision on divorce was that once the marriage itself had come to an end there should, as far as possible, be a clean break financially. For this reason the courts are required to settle financial matters by way of payment of a **lump sum** and/or **property transfer order** and only impose payment of periodical allowance where lump sums and/or property transfer orders are inappropriate or insuffi- cient. Periodical allowance can only be awarded under the third to fifth principles listed above. 'Periodical allowance' is the name for weekly or monthly payments ordered by the court to be paid by one spouse to the other where there is not enough capital or other property to give the spouse claiming financial provision a fair share of the matrimonial property. It is paid out of the paying spouse's earnings. The amount can be increased or decreased on a material change in circumstances. Payment can be for a certain length of time or for an indefinite time but always ends on the death or re-marriage of the spouse receiving the periodical allowance. If the paying spouse dies the obligation to pay continues against his estate but his executors can ask the court to terminate the order.

It will be seen that the court has very wide powers and discretion to re-distribute the matrimonial property in such a way as to achieve a settlement which is justified by the five principles above and reasonable having regard to the parties' resources at the time of the divorce.

Each case turns on its own facts and circumstances and every case is dealt with individually. The outcome of a friend's or relative's case is no guide to what would happen in your own situation. The court can look at decisions made in previous cases for guidance in current cases.

Orders the court can make

- payment of a capital sum;
- a property transfer order;
- payment of periodical allowance;
- a pension earmarking order;
- an incidental order.

Capital sum

This can be ordered to be paid in a lump sum, from savings or the proceeds of sale of property, or by instalments. Payment of a capital sum can also be used to replace periodical allowance where there has been a material change in circumstances.

An order for a capital sum can only be made where the payer has resources from which to meet it. These do not necessarily have to be existing resources. For example, if the court is satisfied that the payer could reasonably be expected to borrow to fund the payment of a capital sum then it can make an order to that effect.

Property transfer order

This can apply to any matrimonial asset which is capable of being transferred under the law of property. It does not cover pensions. Most commonly it is used to transfer ownership of the matrimonial home from either joint names or the name of one spouse, to the other. It can also be used to transfer endowment policies, shares, motor vehicles, etc. Where spouses live in rented accommodation one spouse can ask the court to transfer the tenancy to their name from joint names or from the name of the other spouse, in terms of the Matrimonial Homes (Family Protection) (Scotland) Act 1981.

Periodical allowance

As we have seen, this will only be ordered under the third to fifth principles listed above, and then only if a capital sum and/or property transfer order are inappropriate or insufficient.

N.B. After separation but before divorce is granted one spouse can claim periodic payments from the other to assist with their day-to-day living expenses. This is called **interim aliment**. In making such an award the court must have regard to the needs and resources of the parties, their earning capacities and generally all the circumstances of the case.

Pension earmarking order

The question of pension rights is probably the most controversial aspect of current divorce legislation. The proportion of pension rights which has built up between the date of the marriage and the relevant date is matrimonial property and in many cases represent a substantial proportion of that property. The value used by the courts is the cash equivalent transfer value of that proportion of the pension at the relevant date. In certain circumstances another basis for valuation might be used. For members of occupational pension schemes the scheme administrator will calculate the **cash equivalent transfer value** on request. Individuals who pay into personal pension schemes can obtain this information from the company operating the scheme.

Earmarking orders were introduced to cover the situation where pension interests formed a substantial part of the matrimonial property and there was insufficient other property to give the spouse without the pension sufficient capital or other property to ensure a fair share of the net value of matrimonial property on divorce.

The classic case would be a couple approaching retirement, living in rented accommodation and with few assets apart from the husband's pension. In such a case the court can order payment of a capital sum to be paid out of the husband's pension lump sum payable to him on his retirement or in respect of his death. The order directs the pension trustees to make payment direct to the other spouse of the whole or part of the lump sum. While this is all very well in theory, in practice it is proving difficult. The order must be worded very carefully. Some pension schemes do not pay out on the death of the pensioner before retirement age, or pay only a small amount which may not be enough to satisfy the earmarking order. Other schemes offer the option of commuting all or part of the lump sum. This means that you can reduce the amount of the lump sum and increase the weekly or monthly payment, which you receive on retirement. If this were done it would defeat the earmarking order.

If the person who has the earmarking order changes their name or address they must give notice of that fact within 14 days of the change. The notice must be sent to the pension administrators by ordinary first class post and is treated as having been received by them on the seventh day following the date of posting.

Pension splitting

This procedure is not yet in force and will require legislation by the Scottish Parliament. Pension splitting would allow the value of one party's pension at the relevant date to be divided and part transferred into a pension scheme for the other spouse. This could be either within the same scheme or into another scheme. This would avoid the difficulties associated with earmarking orders.

Incidental orders

These include:

- an order for sale of property;
- an order for valuation of property;
- an order regulating occupation of the matrimonial home;
- an order regulating liability between the parties for outgoings in respect of the matrimonial home;
- any other order which the court thinks is appropriate or necessary to give effect to the five basic principles outlined above

or to give effect to any order for payment of a capital sum or periodical allowance or for a property transfer order or pension earmarking order.

Orders regulating occupation of the matrimonial home and liability for outgoings can only be granted on or after divorce. These are most commonly used to allow the spouse who has care of the children to remain in the matrimonial home until the youngest child is 16 when the property can then be sold and the proceeds divided in accordance with whatever order has been made for payment of a capital sum. In practice couples prefer to avoid the use of this provision where possible as it can cause problems. The purpose of these incidental orders is to enable the court to have as wide powers as possible to fashion a settlement specifically adapted to the particular circumstances of the individual case.

COURT ORDERS – PROTECTION AND ENFORCEMENT

Protection

In divorce proceedings you can obtain orders for your spouse to provide details of their income and other resources. You can also recover documents from third parties, such as banks, building societies and company registrars, to obtain information about your spouse's money, bank accounts and shares, etc. If you have reason to believe that your spouse may dispose of assets to try to thwart your claim for financial provision you can obtain court orders allowing you to arrest (freeze) their bank or building society accounts or funds due to them held by other parties. You can also prevent them from making a voluntary disposal of heritable property (e.g. a house, flat or piece of ground) by a procedure known as inhibition. You can also obtain interdict.

If, within one year of being divorced, you discover that within the five years before the divorce was started your spouse transferred or sold property, thereby defeating in whole or part your claim for financial provision, you can ask the court to cancel the transaction or make any other order that it sees fit. If a third party has bought the property from your spouse at a fair price and did not know about your claim then that party's rights cannot be prejudiced. In practical terms this means that the court would not cancel the transaction but it could make an order for your spouse to make a payment to you in lieu.

Enforcement

Periodical allowance, interim aliment and aliment for children

If a spouse fails to pay any of the above, the order can be enforced by arrestment. You can arrest bank and building society accounts, or any other money in the hands of third parties, which is due to your spouse. Wages can be arrested by earnings arrestment. A current maintenance arrestment is available to deal with persistent maintenance defaulters. This recovers current maintenance each week or month as it falls due, by deduction from the defaulter's wages. The amount that can be deducted depends on the level of the spouse's earnings and may be less than the actual amount of the order.

Capital sum

Again, you can use arrestment and earnings arrestment. Where the capital sum is more than £1,500 you can petition for your spouse's bankruptcy. Poinding and warrant sale of possessions can also be used but this is not commonly done in practice, as the amount realised is often insufficient to justify the expense involved.

DOMESTIC VIOLENCE

The Matrimonial Homes (Family Protection) (Scotland) Act 1981 provides protection from domestic violence for married couples and, in some limited circumstances, for heterosexual cohabiting couples. Prior to the passing of this Act the spouse in whose name title to the home was taken or in whose name the property was rented could effectively put the other spouse out on the street.

The Act provides that where one spouse is the owner or tenant of the property (called the **entitled spouse**) and the other (called the **non-entitled spouse**) is not, then the non entitled spouse has the right to continue to live in the property together with any children of the family. If the other spouse has already forced the non-entitled spouse out they have the right to come back and live in the house together with the children.

'Matrimonial home' is defined very broadly. It includes any house, caravan, houseboat or other structure which has been provided as or has become a family residence. You do not need to have lived in the property together or to have children in order to fall within the definition.

The non-entitled spouse has the right, without the consent of the entitled spouse, to pay the rent or mortgage and endowment premiums and to carry out essential repairs to the property. The non-entitled spouse can also apply to the court for an order sharing liability for these costs between the spouses. Where the non-entitled spouse has no income and the entitled spouse is earning the court could order them to pay all of these costs. You can also get this order where the home is owned or tenanted jointly, in other words where **both** spouses are entitled.

A non-entitled spouse can apply to the court for orders:

- declaring and/or enforcing their occupancy rights in the property;
- restricting the other spouse's occupancy rights;
- regulating the exercise of either spouse's occupancy rights;
- protecting their occupancy rights in relation to the other spouse.

These orders can also be obtained by either spouse if both entitled for example joint tenants. In making such orders the court must consider the following factors:

- the conduct of the spouses towards each other and otherwise;
- the respective needs and financial resources of the spouses;
- the needs of any child of the family;
- whether the house is used in connection with a trade, business or profession of either spouse;
- whether the entitled spouse offers or has offered to make available to the non-entitled spouse any suitable alternative accommodation.

In practice these orders are not often sought, with the exception of declarator of occupancy rights which is usually sought as a necessary along with an exclusion order.

Exclusion orders

The 1981 Act gives the court power to **exclude** either spouse
from the matrimonial home. Generally, an exclusion order will be
granted only if there has been violence by one spouse against the
other or the children of the family. The court has to be satisfied
that the exclusion order is necessary for the protection of the
applicant spouse or any child of the family from any behaviour of
the non-applicant spouse which is causing or would cause injury
to the physical or mental health of the applicant or the child. This
includes threats of further behaviour as well as actual behaviour.
The court must not make the order if it would be unjustified or
unreasonable in all the circumstances of the case, including the
factors listed above. Orders can be granted on an urgent interim
basis.

The court can also grant an order for **ejection** of the non-applicant spouse, which can be enforced by sheriff officers, if the non-
applicant spouse refuses to obey the exclusion order and move
out of the house voluntarily. The non-applicant spouse can also
be **interdicted** from entering the house without the applicant
spouse's permission and from removing household contents.

An exclusion order is a very effective remedy which deprives a
person of the right to occupy their own home. The courts will not
grant it lightly and must be satisfied that it is necessary to protect
the applicant spouse or a child of the family. In the absence of
physical violence you must show that your spouse's presence is
causing injury to your mental health or that of a child of the
marriage. Distress caused by a tense or unpleasant atmosphere
within the home, because of marital difficulties, will not in itself
be enough.

Matrimonial interdicts

One spouse could always obtain a common law interdict against molestation by the other. Difficulty arose if the interdict was breached (i.e. disobeyed). The police had no power to arrest the spouse alleged to have committed the breach unless they had committed a criminal offence, such as assault. The only option available to the spouse holding the interdict was to raise another court action for breach of interdict. The 1981 Act gave the courts the power to attach a **power of arrest** to what were defined as **matrimonial interdicts**. These are interdicts restraining or prohibiting any conduct of one spouse towards the other spouse or a child of the family or prohibiting a spouse from entering or remaining in a matrimonial home or a specified area in the vicinity of the home.

When such an interdict is granted the court **must** attach a power of arrest to it unless it appears to the court that in all the circumstances the power of arrest is unnecessary. Where a matrimonial interdict is granted as part of an exclusion order the court **must** attach the power of arrest if asked to by the applicant spouse.

Where there is a matrimonial interdict with a power of arrest attached a police constable may arrest the spouse without warrant if he has reasonable cause to believe that he is in breach of the interdict. A complaint from the spouse who has been awarded the interdict is sufficient to create reasonable cause in most situations.

Once arrested, the spouse against whom the interdict has been granted (referred to below as 'the offending spouse') may be released by the officer in charge of a police station but only if that officer is satisfied that there is no likelihood of violence to the other spouse or any child of the family. The police must also report the facts to the procurator fiscal who can decide whether to prosecute the offending spouse in a criminal court.

If the police detain the offending spouse and the procurator fiscal decides that there is to be no criminal prosecution the offending spouse must be brought before the sheriff in the sheriff court on the next available court day. The procurator fiscal must tell the other spouse and their solicitor that criminal proceedings are not being taken. The procurator fiscal may then ask the court to detain the non-applicant spouse for a further period of up to two days. The sheriff can do so, if he is satisfied that on the face of it:

- there has been a breach of the interdict;

- proceedings for breach of interdict will be taken; and

- there is a substantial risk of violence by the non-applicant spouse against the applicant spouse or a child of the family.

Power of arrest has made interdict remain a useful order, as the spouse who has the order can expect a prompt response from the police if it is breached. The spouse against whom the order is held is more likely to think twice about breaching it, knowing that they could face up to three nights in a police cell.

Non-harassment orders

These are available under the Protection from Harassment Act 1997 which was introduced to deal with the phenomenon of stalking. A non-harassment order can be obtained by any individual against another and is not restricted to husbands and wives or cohabitees. These orders can be useful where the behaviour complained of may not justify an interdict. If such an order is breached then the person breaching it can be punished in the criminal courts by imprisonment or fine. In addition the victim of the harassment may also be awarded damages both for anxiety caused by the harassment and for any financial loss which has resulted from it.

Immediate action

If you have suffered **actual physical violence**, or the **threat** of it, you should call the police if necessary and seek medical treatment for any injuries, recording with the hospital or your G.P. how the injury was sustained. You should then consult a solicitor for advice on obtaining an interdict, power of arrest, exclusion order and/or non-harassment order. Note that a cohabitee can only obtain a matrimonial interdict with power of arrest attached if they are either the non-entitled partner (i.e. the property is owned or rented in the violent partner's name) or if both partners are entitled to occupy the property (i.e. owned or rented in joint names). This is a defect in the Act. Couples who are not married and are not living together cannot obtain a matrimonial interdict with power of arrest and are only entitled to the protection of a common law interdict.

A spouse who obtains a matrimonial interdict with power of arrest loses the protection of the power of arrest when the parties divorce.

You cannot obtain a matrimonial interdict with power of arrest against an ex-spouse.

The Scottish Parliament is currently considering reform of the law in this area and in particular it has been proposed that matrimonial interdicts with power of arrest should be extended in their fullest form to former spouses and cohabitees and re-named 'domestic interdicts'.

9 Death

All of us, at some time, may have to deal with the consequences of a death in the family. The loss of a loved one has many legal consequences and, as we will see, if the deceased left some indication of their wishes then matters can be made more straightforward. This chapter therefore deals with registering a death, financial matters and making a will.

REGISTERING A DEATH

Natural causes

When a death occurs due to natural causes the doctor who attended the deceased during their final illness will issue a medical certificate, free of charge, certifying the cause of death. You must register the death within eight days with the Registrar of Births, Deaths and Marriages in the area in which the death took place. The Registrar's address will be in the local telephone directory. You will need to take along the medical certificate and be in a position to provide details about the deceased. The minimum you will need is the deceased's full name, address, age, place of birth and details of any marriage or divorce. The Registrar will ask whether the deceased was in receipt of any State pensions. The death will be recorded and a certified copy of the entry, called the death certificate, is issued. You should ask for several copies of the death certificate, as these may well be needed to show to banks and other people who hold assets of the deceased. It is cheaper to order the certificates all at the same time.

Fatal accidents

If the death was due to a sudden or unexplained cause there may require to be a further medical examination, called a **post mortem**, carried out under the supervision of a pathologist. This will also happen if the death was due to an accident while the deceased was undergoing surgery or in the custody of the police. If the examination establishes that the death was not due to natural causes then a **fatal accident inquiry** will be held before a sheriff. Relatives and other interested parties are entitled to be legally represented at such an inquiry and if the death was due to an accident at work then interested bodies such as trade unions can also appear. Scotland has no equivalent of the English coroner; all of these procedures are under the control of the criminal public prosecutor called the procurator fiscal.

Death abroad

Deaths abroad must be registered in the country where they occurred, according to any local rules. You should also try to have the death registered with the local British Consul. He will be able to give you advice on procedures for bringing the body home. You should also try to obtain translations of any foreign documents which are issued. You will require the death certificate or whatever equivalent has been issued in order to bring the body through British Customs. You will then require to register the foreign death certificate with the Registrar of the district where the deceased lived in this country. In the event that the death happened during an organised holiday, the travel insurers should provide full assistance with all the legal formalities of bringing the deceased's body home.

THE FUNERAL

When drafting a will, most Scottish solicitors will have asked the deceased if they had any special directions in connection with their funeral. You should therefore check as soon as possible to see if the deceased has left a will or other funeral instructions. The cost of a funeral can be very high and you should be clear with the funeral director who is to be legally responsible for paying the bill. If you are arranging the funeral on behalf of someone else, you must ensure that you do not accept liability for the funeral director's invoice and that, if possible, you arrange for the person who is paying the bill to see the funeral director personally before the final arrangements are made. There are a number of pre-paid funeral plans and insurance schemes to cover funeral expenses and it is well worth investigating whether the deceased might have subscribed to one of these. You can also obtain assistance from the DSS if the deceased has left nothing with which to pay for the funeral.

IMMEDIATE FINANCIAL CONSEQUENCES

Once a bank or building society learns of a customer's death all their accounts there are automatically frozen unless held in joint names with someone still alive, with only one signature needed to operate the account. Many banks and building societies open joint accounts with what is called a **survivorship clause**, which basically means that the account holders have agreed, as a matter of contract, that on the death of either party all the funds in the account will be transferred automatically to the person left alive. Such accounts do not therefore need any other legal formality to pass to the survivor; all that the bank or building society will require is to see the death certificate. However, legal authority is necessary to collect in the assets of a deceased person that were not held jointly with anyone else and this is what is generally referred to as **winding up the deceased's estate**.

The first thing that must be established is whether the deceased left a will. A will is a person's written declaration of what they want done with their assets on their death. We will see later that the law does make some restrictions on the deceased's freedom to hand over their assets in a will but, generally speaking, we all have the right to make whatever provision we wish on our death. It is therefore essential to go through any papers or documents left by the deceased to see if a will can be found. You should also check to see if there are any clues as to where a will might be lodged. Wills are often held by solicitors and sometimes by banks and you may find an invoice or other correspondence which will point the way to someone holding a will.

We can make as many wills as we wish during our lives and it is the **last** will, i.e. the one dated most recently before death, that matters. It is usually considered wise to destroy previous wills when making a new one but it is not legally necessary and any previous wills which have been kept are simply treated as if they did not exist. However if there were an older will and for some reason the last dated will was declared to be invalid, our legal system considers it to be undesirable that the wishes of the deceased be totally ignored and the older will will then be used.

You must also preserve other official documents carefully as these may not only be relevant to the financial affairs of the deceased but may require to be returned to the issuing authorities. A passport should be returned to the Passport Office and any driving licence should be returned to the DVLC at Swansea. You should ensure that all credit cards are destroyed or returned and the companies advised of the death in case of any error or fraud on the accounts. Insurance policies generally require to be returned to the issuing companies, together with any claim forms.

Once you have found the last will, the winding up of the estate follows the rules of **testate succession**. This is in contrast to winding up an estate where the deceased has left no will, which follows the rules of **intestate succession**.

TESTATE SUCCESSION

Executors

The will must appoint persons to carry out the deceased's wishes. These people are called executors and as they have been nominated by the deceased in the will they are called **executors nominate**. The deceased may have failed to nominate executors in his will or they could have died before the deceased. In these cases if the will leaves everything to one person (called the general disponee or universal legatee) or if someone has been left the remainder of a deceased's estate after he has given specific items to friends and relatives (called the residuary legatee) then these persons can become the executors.

Obtaining authority to act

The executors do not have the power to collect in assets simply
by producing the will. They require the authority of the court
which in Scotland is called **confirmation** (in England, probate).
An inventory of all that the deceased owned must be drawn up
on a special form issued by the court and this is presented to the
sheriff clerk of the local sheriff court. There are fees to be paid for
the sheriff clerk's work and the original will must be produced.
The clerk will then issue the confirmation document, which is the
order of the court to the executors to collect in the assets and lists
what all of those assets are. For a small extra fee, the sheriff clerk
can be asked to issue individual certificates for items of property.
This is particularly useful if the deceased left a number of individual assets, for example bank or building society accounts, as each
institution will require to see the executors' authority before it will
hand over the deceased's funds. If you had to send the whole confirmation document to each bank or building society it could take
weeks or even months to collect in all the money. It is more
sensible to send individual certificates as hopefully then all the
funds will come in at more or less the same time.

Small estates

A simple procedure for obtaining confirmation to small estates
exists where the assets (after deduction of any valid debts) do not
exceed £17,000. The sheriff clerk will then assist in filling up the
inventory and all other formalities, for a modest fee. This procedure applies whether the deceased left a will or not. You may also
find that where the estate is very small, assets can be uplifted by
simply producing the death certificate and signing a declaration

that you are the person paying the funeral account or are the next-of-kin. Banks, insurance companies and the like usually have their own guidelines as to how much they will consider a small estate, and will have their own forms of declaration to be signed.

Inheritance tax

If the value of the deceased's assets (less the debts) is more than £234,000 then inheritance tax must be paid. The inventory which is sent to the sheriff clerk must therefore be sent to the Inland Revenue to assess the tax due. You cannot obtain confirmation to a deceased's estate (with or without a will) unless the inheritance tax has been paid. It is important to understand this before embarking upon applying for confirmation because you will not be able to use the deceased's frozen assets to pay the tax. You may have to obtain an overdraft or bank loan to do so. This is one of the reasons why executors cannot be compelled to serve if they do not want to. Before accepting office as executor you should take legal or other qualified advice if you believe that there is any question of inheritance tax being due.

General administration

Once the executors are confirmed to the estate it is their duty to gather in the assets of the deceased and then to pass them on or sell them in accordance with the deceased's wishes as set out in the will, or to divide everything up in accordance with the legal rules which apply where there is no will. There is a great deal that an active executor can do for themselves but generally legal or other qualified advice will be necessary where:

- the deceased left:

- land, including houses or flats;

- rented properties;

- assets abroad;

- children aged under 18;

- the estate has more debts than assets;

- missing beneficiaries must be traced;

- claims are made against the estate by people who are not mentioned in the will.

This is not an exhaustive list and executors should take advice on any matter which causes them concern but the most likely difficulty will be claims against the estate. These can be from persons who believe they that had some claim against the deceased before he died, for example from an accident or an unpaid debt, or from the family of the deceased claiming rights conferred on them by the law.

Third party claims

The executor represents the deceased and any debt or other financial claim that could have been brought against the deceased before his death can be brought against the executor. The executor is not personally liable and pays claims from the assets of the deceased's estate. The executor must therefore pay all debts lawfully due by the deceased first and only then can he consider the instructions of the deceased in the will and any claims made by the family. It is for this reason that an executor cannot be compelled to hand over any assets of the deceased until after the expiry of a period of six months from the date of death. This is to allow for claims to be considered properly. Once the six-month period has passed (or, of course, earlier if he is sure of the debt position) the executor can proceed to distribute the estate to beneficiaries and family and he will not be answerable to anyone who comes after the six-month period, claiming that the deceased owed him a debt. This rule is to protect executors who have acted in good faith and there can be exceptions, for example where the executor ignored plain evidence that the debts exceeded the assets and just paid whoever he liked best. Even after the six-month period, if the executor still has assets in his control someone who validly claims a debt after the six months is entitled to be paid. After the debts have been met the executor turns to distribution, either under the will or by the rules of intestate succession.

Implementing the will

Gifts of individual assets in a will are called **legacies** or bequests. These may be sums of money or items, for example jewellery. Everything that is left over after legacies have been paid or handed over is called **residue**. The executor collects in all that is left and either turns it into cash or hands over the assets to whoever has been left the residue. The family, however, has claims on the deceased's estate, no matter what he has said in his will. This can arise in two ways: first, the deceased may have simply cut out his spouse or children or, secondly, have left them something but not what they wanted and they refuse to accept the legacy. A widow or widower can claim one third of the moveable estate (cash and most other items other than land or houses) if there are children, and one half of it if there are none. These rights are called the *jus relictae* (for a widow) and *jus relicti* (for a widower). Children are collectively entitled to claim one third of the moveable estate to share between them if there is a widow or widower, and one half if there is none. This right is called *legitim* or the 'bairns' part'.

INTESTATE SUCCESSION

The lack of a will, whether because the deceased did not make one or because the one made is declared invalid after the deceased's death (see Wills, p. 250) means that the law must intervene to say who gets the deceased's assets.

The court must first of all be asked to authorise executors to act in exactly the same way as if there were a will. Several types of people can ask to be appointed. To distinguish these executors from those appointed under a will, they are called **executors dative**. The usual order of preference would be the widow or widower, then the children or other direct descendants. However creditors and even the local procurator fiscal can be appointed if necessary.

The procedure for obtaining confirmation is precisely the same as where there is a valid will but when the inventory of assets is presented to the sheriff clerk this is accompanied by a written application which sets out why the executor dative should be appointed. An executor dative can also be required by the court to obtain an insurance bond for the value of the assets.

Once the executor dative has the assets under his control he is then required to pass these on to the family under a fixed set of rules set out in the Succession (Scotland) Act 1964. The widow or widower is entitled to a first claim called **prior rights**. These consist of:

- the matrimonial home, to the value of £130,000;

- the furniture and contents of that home, to the value of £22,000;
- cash remaining in the estate, up to £35,000 if there are children, or up to £58,000 if there are none.

These figures are reviewed by the government from time to time and the last revision was on 1 April 1999.

The assets that remain are then divided between the widow or widower and the children and this division is called **legal rights**. The widow or widower is entitled to one third of the moveable assets if there are children and to one half if there are none. The children take one third of the moveable estate where there is a widow or widower and one half where there is none. What remains after prior and legal rights have been taken is called the 'dead's part' or **free estate**. This is claimed by the next-of-kin, in the following priority, until an heir or heirs are found:

- children (or grandchildren, and so on down);
- parents and brothers or sisters (if both then each class shares 50 per cent of the estate);
- brothers and sisters, if no parents alive;
- parents, if no brothers or sisters alive;
- widow or widower;
- uncles and aunts (both maternal and paternal);
- grandparents;
- grandparents' brothers and sisters;
- great grandparents, and so on upwards.

If there are no claimants from the family at all then the estate passes to the Crown, on the basis that the State represents the ultimate 'family' connection.

WILLS

Making a will

Anyone over the age of 12 in Scotland may make a will and it is certainly advisable to do so if you have any assets which you wish to pass on to specific people or if you wish to avoid your assets passing to the government because you have no family to claim them. It can be a risky business to make a will without some kind of qualified advice and many home-made wills are declared to be invalid for one reason or another. The basic requirements of a good will are **clarity** and **simplicity**. A checklist should be made of what it is you want to do and you should then say it in the simplest possible terms. You should identify any specific items clearly and avoid general terms such as 'jewellery' or 'ornaments'. The structure of a good will should therefore be as follows:

- set out your full name and address;

- state that you are making your last will and testament to settle the succession to your estate on your death;

- you should appoint executors, giving their full names, occupations and addresses. It is advisable to appoint at least two and preferably more executors to ensure that at least one will be available to carry out your wishes on your death;

- you should direct that your executors settle all your lawful debts and obligations;

- you should give any directions you wish as to your funeral arrangements;

- you should make any specific gifts, clearly identifying the items and giving the name and address of the person to whom they are to pass;

- you must then divide up what is left (the residue) to the person or persons you wish to have it, giving their full names and addresses;

- you should state whether you wish the residue or share of residue of anyone you have named to pass to their heirs (e.g. spouse or children) if they are not alive at the date of your death. If you do not make such a provision then that share will simply pass to anyone else who is sharing in the residue;

- you should make a final provision that if all the people you have mentioned in the will (or their heirs if you have said that they can inherit instead of their parents, etc.) are dead then you wish your estate to go to a specified charity. This will at least mean that your assets go to some use that you approve of rather than passing to the government;

- sign the will on every page, date it and get it witnessed.

Signing formalities

New rules for the signing of wills came into force in August 1995. A will should be clear and legible but it does not need to be typed. It must still be signed on each page but only one witness is required, as opposed to the former rule which demanded two. In England the witness must not be a person who is benefiting under the will but there is no such rule in Scotland. It would be considered good practice to avoid using a beneficiary as the witness but it would not make the will invalid. Blind people must have the will read over to them by a notary public who then signs the will on their behalf and adds a statement of who he is and his authority to act. This requires to be witnessed in the normal manner.

Challenging a will

The making of a will is meant to prevent squabbling over the deceased's assets but there are rules that allow a will, which seems to be valid, to be challenged:

- the deceased did not know or understand what he or she was doing when making the will, due to some mental incapacity;

- the deceased may have been subject to undue influence or fraud into making provision for someone in a will when they would not otherwise have done so;

- the will may not be the last will and a later will is produced;

- the will did not make provision for a child born after the date it was signed (*conditio si testator sine liberis decesserit*). This challenge is based on a presumption that the deceased could not have intended that the will should remain in force due to the changed circumstances, and would have wished that the child should benefit. The best illustration of the likely application of this rule is where the deceased was childless when the will was made and then died shortly after a child is born. However, if it can be proved that the deceased **deliberately** left out the child then the will would stand;

- a specific legacy or direction in the will can also be challenged even though the will itself is declared valid. This occurs where the bequest or direction is impossible to implement, too vague, illegal or contrary to the public good. A bequest to a wife provided that she never re-marries is unlawful, so she gets the inheritance and the condition is ignored. Equally, a direction that money should be used to erect a 400-foot statue of the deceased on the Esplanade of Edinburgh Castle is likely to be declared contrary to the public good and therefore not carried out.

LEGAL TERMS

The law of inheritance has developed over many centuries, with complexities beyond the scope of this work but a number of technical terms may be encountered which it is useful to define. The Glossary (see p. 263) contains other definitions which are relevant to this chapter but the following are of direct application:

- **special destination:** this is a direction stating what is to happen to an asset if it does not pass to the person or persons that were originally directed to have it, for example a bequest to A but failing him to B;

- **per capita** or **per stirpes:** these terms describe the alternative schemes of division where bequests are made to groups rather than individuals. This is best explained by an example: where a deceased left a will sharing the estate between three children but they had themselves died and their shares were passing to the deceased's grandchildren, if the division was *per capita* then each grandchild would take an equal share of the assets but if divided *per stirpes* the assets would be divided in three and each line of grandchildren would share one third between them;

- **liferent:** a bequest of the use of an asset for the beneficiary's lifetime after which it passes to whoever the deceased has stated should own it, for example the use of a house by a widow for as long as she lives and thereafter to pass to the children.

Securing your Rights in the Sheriff Court

10

Scotland is divided into six regional sheriffdoms providing some 50 sheriff courts. In major cities each courthouse may accommodate several courtrooms while in country districts there may be only one. The sheriff is a judge with considerable authority who may hear virtually all civil cases no matter what the value. All qualified lawyers may appear to present cases in the sheriff court. A sheriff clerk (who deals with the administration and paperwork of a case) and a bar officer (who looks after practical matters such as bringing in witnesses and keeping order) will assist the sheriff.

HOW DOES THE CASE PROGRESS?

The sheriff court has three main forms of procedure.

All actions for sums in excess of £1,500, or for important matters such as divorce or other family actions, are called **ordinary actions**.

The other two procedures – the **summary cause** and the **small claim** – can be used for any dispute, including eviction of tenants and husband/wife maintenance claims, provided that any money sought is within the financial limits. A small claim is only for sums up to and including £750 and a summary cause covers claims valued at over £750, up to and including £1,500. Note: at the time of writing the Scottish Parliament is considering regulations which will increase the small claim limit to £1,500.00 and the Ordinary limit to £5,000.00. The draft regulations also provide for the option of raising personal injury actions (which can have complicated issues which make a simpler procedure inappropriate (see Accidents, p. 37) under the ordinary rules even if the claim is less than £5,000.00

All Scottish cases call the party making the claim the **pursuer** and the party defending the **defender**.

SUMMARY CAUSES AND SMALL CLAIMS

Summary cause and small claim procedures are largely similar. The details of the claim are set out on a pre-printed form provided by the court. A date is set for the case to call before the sheriff if either the claim is not admitted or the debtor does admit the claim but wishes to pay by instalments. The sheriff tries to resolve matters at the calling and must do so if the dispute relates only to paying off the debt by instalments. Where there is still dispute on the facts the sheriff may need to hear evidence, in which case he will fix another date for the parties to return with witnesses and any documentary evidence. The procedures are reasonably simple and paperwork is meant to be kept to the minimum to enable the parties to bring or defend such cases without the assistance of lawyers if they wish.

However, even if the procedure is simple, the legal issues can be complex and no one should undertake such cases without some professional advice. The expenses recoverable under these procedures are very limited.

ORDINARY ACTIONS

The main procedure in the sheriff court commences with the issue of a summons called an **initial writ**. This is drafted individually to suit the facts of the pursuer's case. The court authorises the writ to be sent to the defender together with directions on how to respond. There are three options for the defender:

- do nothing, in which case the court will hold the claim to have been proved and will grant the orders sought by the pursuer. In matrimonial cases the court will still want some further evidence, including statements on the welfare of children where appropriate, but these are generally submitted in writing without the parties having to appear before the sheriff;

- admit the claim but ask the court to do something for the defender, for example allow time to pay a debt. The pursuer will be asked whether this is acceptable. If it is, the court will grant the order sought by the pursuer, subject to what was asked for by the defender. If the pursuer objects, the court will fix a hearing to decide whether or not to grant the order sought by the defender;

- defend. The action then follows what is known as ordinary standard procedure.

Ordinary standard procedure

The clerk of court fixes a series of dates by which stages of procedure must be complete.

The defender must lodge his answer to the claim in writing and the pursuer may respond to what his opponent has said. This written account of the case is called the **pleadings**.

The next time the case will call before the sheriff is on the date fixed for an **options hearing**. At this hearing the sheriff is required to try to ensure that procedure now moves swiftly to a point where a decision on the dispute is made. The parties may not have had sufficient time to put all their points in writing and either side can ask for a continuation to enable it to do so. In very complex cases the court can grant a long continuation of up to eight weeks which is called additional procedure. If the dispute relates only to facts then the sheriff will order a hearing with witnesses, which is called a **proof**. There may be technical legal issues to be decided (perhaps to consider if a claim has been brought within time limits which the law lays down in some cases; for example, see Accidents, p. 37) and in that case the sheriff will fix a **debate**. The court may still order a proof after the debate if the technical point raised is not successful.

Once a proof is fixed, parties must exchange lists of documents they wish to rely on in court, and the names and addresses of any witnesses.

FAMILY ACTIONS

There are many special rules about actions relating to family matters, which your lawyer will explain to you. In actions relating to divorce or children the court can require parties to attempt to mediate their problems before the case proceeds further. Issues such as who should pay legal expenses are less easily defined because the terms 'winner' or 'loser' are not appropriate. The court can also appoint separate lawyers to represent children if their interests seem to conflict with those of their parents or guardians who are disputing their future.

PROOF

This is the hearing of evidence, both oral and documentary, before the sheriff. Generally, the pursuer's lawyer will start, leading all his witnesses and any physical evidence he thinks will persuade the court that the pursuer should win. The defender's lawyer will then **cross-examine**, or ask the pursuer's witnesses questions to try to expose weakness or inconsistency in the pursuer's evidence, and put the defender's case to the pursuer's witnesses for their comment. The defender's witnesses will then be led and they can be cross-examined by the pursuer's lawyer. Each side will make a speech called a **submission** and the sheriff will then adjourn the hearing in order to make a **written judgement**. In complex cases the judge may take months to prepare his judgement but an average of six to eight weeks must be expected.

WHAT HAPPENS IF I LOSE?

You may have to pay the legal expenses of your opponent unless you have insurance to cover such costs. There are special expenses rules for parties who are covered by legal aid which may reduce liability perhaps even to nil. You will obviously have your own lawyer's bill to pay unless you are receiving legal aid, covered by insurance or have agreed with your lawyer that no fee will be payable should you lose your case. If you are an individual (not a partnership or limited company) and have been ordered to pay a sum of money less than £10,000 you can apply for time to pay.

Your lawyer will also advise if you have any prospect of appeal. The decision of a sheriff can be appealed to the sheriff principal and then to the Court of Session, with a final appeal to the House of Lords on legal points only. The issue before an appeal court is why the decision of the lower court might be **legally** wrong, and this is dealt with by highly skilled and technical argument.

WHAT HAPPENS IF I WIN?

Your opponent has a right of appeal and may choose to exercise it. The losing party can seek time to pay where the sum due does not exceed £10,000, provided that the opponent is not a partnership or company. The court hears the parties on any offer to pay by instalments and the sheriff can accept the offer, reject it or fix instalments at a higher level than offered. If the loser does not appeal (and your case is not about payment of money) then that will be the end of the matter. You will receive a copy of the court order (called an **extract decree**) to keep for future reference.

ENFORCEMENT OF DECREES

A court order for payment of money, if not paid voluntarily, must be enforced by one of a number of procedures known collectively as **diligence**. There are four main forms of diligence:

Arrestment

An order to seize money held in the debtor's bank accounts or other cash funds which may be due to the debtor by a third party. This can be done either at the start of the action or after decree has been granted.

Inhibition

An order which stops the debtor from selling land or houses (called heritable assets) or borrowing money on such assets. This can be used at anytime after the start of the action or after decree has been granted.

Poinding and warrant sale

The process of seizing goods such as motor vehicles, machinery and furniture belonging to the debtor and having them sold. This can be done only after decree has been granted.

Sequestration (bankruptcy)

A separate court action founding on the non-payment of the decree in your favour as evidence of bankruptcy. The court appoints a trustee to take control of all the assets of the debtor in order to sell them off to raise funds. The trustee must divide any money recovered between all creditors and the creditor holding the decree will receive only a share (called a dividend). Many debtors do pay in full before the final order to avoid the consequences of bankruptcy.

COMPLAINTS

You may have some complaint about how your case was handled by your lawyer, your opponent's lawyer or even the court administration. Complaints about how the court system dealt with you (perhaps persistently fixing hearings on days when the court had too much business to hear your case) should be made to:

Scottish Court Service
Hayweight House
23 Lauriston Street
Edinburgh.

Complaints about solicitors should be made to:

The Law Society of Scotland
26–27 Drumsheugh Gardens
Edinburgh.

The Law Society will only investigate a complaint against your opponent's solicitor if your own lawyer believes that there was misconduct. The facts that your opponent's solicitor represented his client forcefully or his tactics irritated you are **not** grounds for complaint.

Complaints about your own solicitor can be made to the client relations partner of his firm and if not resolved by this method can be passed to the Law Society of Scotland. These procedures are additional to your right to sue your lawyer for breach of contract or negligence which may have caused you loss.

The Law Society of Scotland is itself scrutinised by the Legal Services Ombudsman who will investigate any allegation that the Society failed to investigate your complaint properly.

II Glossary

SCOTTISH LEGAL TERMS AND LATIN MAXIMS

The following list attempts to define, in plain English, some phrases which appear in this book and others which readers may come across in legal deeds or documents.

a coelo usque ad centrum from the sky to the centre of the earth: this theoretically describes the measure to which a plot of land extends upwards and downwards, but the concept is now qualified by planning and other legislation.

a fortiori by a stronger argument: a phrase used to emphasise the strength of an argument by contrasting it with an earlier weaker one.

a mensa et thoro from bed and board: used to describe the judicial separation of husband and wife.

a morte testatoris from the death of the testator: describes a bequest payable immediately to the beneficiary as opposed to one postponed to a later date, for example until the beneficiary reaches a stated age.

a non domino from one who is not the owner: when land is sold by a lawful occupier but all trace of the identity of the true owner has been lost; the purchaser's defective title is cured by passage of time.

a posteriori viewed from after; reasoning from effect to cause.

a priori viewed from before; reasoning from cause to effect.

ab initio from the beginning.

ab intestato from a person dying intestate; description of property acquired according to the rules of intestate succession.

abbreviate an abstract of a writ and warrant recorded in an official register in bankruptcy proceedings to give public notice thereof.

absolutely insolvent the state of a debtor whose liabilities are greater than his assets.

accession (1) the natural or industrial addition to existing property (e.g. by reproduction or building); (2) an arrangement set out in a deed approved by the creditors of an insolvent person as an alternative to **sequestration**.

Accountant in Bankruptcy the official supervising the administration of sequestration (bankruptcy).

Accountant of Court the officer of the Supreme Court supervising the conduct of persons appointed by the court to look after the financial affairs of others.

acquiescence defence to a claim which arises through failure of a person whose rights have been infringed to object within a reasonable time after he became aware of the facts.

acquirenda assets acquired by a bankrupt after the effective date of his **sequestration**.

act and warrant in **sequestration**, a judicial order confirming the appointment of a permanent trustee in terms of the Bankruptcy (Scotland) Act 1985.

actio quanti minoris an action in Roman law whereby the purchaser of defective goods could seek from the seller the difference between the actual value of the goods and the value they should have had under the contract. This was formally brought into Scots law by the Contract (Scotland) Act 1997.

ad factum praestandum for the performance of an act. A court order which requires the performance or fulfilment of some physical rather than financial obligation, for example to restore a damaged wall.

ad interim in the meantime; a temporary order.

ad longum at length; used of documents or statements quoted in full, as opposed to a summary or extract.

ad valorem according to value, for example stamp duty fixed as a percentage of a house price.

adjudication (1) (generally) the decision of a judge or arbiter; (2) the means by which the Court of Session vests a title to land in a claimant or hands over the heritable **property** of a debtor in security or in satisfaction of a debt to a creditor; (3) a decision by the Inland Revenue Commissioners on stamp duties.

adjust to alter the written **pleadings** in a case during an initial authorised period. This does not need the court's permission and the parties exchange such adjustments without lodging them in court – the court sees them when adjustment is closed, when the final version is then lodged. See **amend**.

admissible evidence testimony given to a court or tribunal which conforms with the legal facts.

advocate (1) a member of the Scottish Bar, the equivalent of the English 'barrister'; (2) a solicitor who is a member of the Society of Advocates in Aberdeen; (3) (verb) to submit the judgement of an inferior court to review by a superior court. In modern practice this procedure is rare and is restricted to criminal jurisdiction.

affidavit a written statement made on oath and signed by the maker, most commonly used in undefended actions of divorce.

affirm (verb) as a witness, to make a solemn declaration to tell the truth, where the maker prefers, for religious or other reasons, not to take the oath.

agnate a person related to another on the father's side; the opposite of **cognate** (related on the mother's side).

aliment provision for maintenance for the support of a spouse or child.

amend to alter the written **pleadings** in an action, only with permission of the court, after the adjustment period is closed, or to alter names and addresses of the parties or what the court is being asked to grant at any time. The court may impose conditions for the right to amend, for example paying a sum in costs to the other side for inconvenience. See **adjust**.

amicus curiae a friend of the court; one who argues at the request or with the leave of the court for an unrepresented party or in the public interest and free of charge.

animo donandi with the intention of giving as a gift.

annuity a right to a yearly payment of money.

ante litem motam before a court action is raised.

apparent insolvency the legal formalities which must be established under the Bankruptcy (Scotland) Act 1985 prior to **sequestration** proceedings by creditors.

appellant a person appealing to a higher court from the decision of a lower court (e.g. in a criminal case from the sheriff court or district court to the High Court of Justiciary, or in a civil case from the Court of Session to the House of Lords).

arbiter a person appointed to adjudicate in a dispute outside the courts. On a question of fact, his decision is final; on a question of law, unless otherwise agreed, he may (on the application of either party) and must (if the Court of Session so directs) state a case for the court's opinion on any question of law.

arrestment the taking or freezing of the property of a debtor which is in the hands of a third party, done to obtain security for a creditor.

ascendant a relative from a previous generation, for example a parent or great-uncle.

ascription the application of payments to debts in a prescribed order. Thus a sum paid by a debtor would be set against interest due before reducing the original debt.

assignation (1) the act of transferring rights to incorporeal moveable property, for example an insurance policy; (2) the document transferring such rights.

assoilzie (verb) to absolve; to make a final decision in a civil action in favour of the defender. The judgement is termed 'absolvitor'.

attestation witnessing of a document.

attorney a person acting on behalf of another with his written authority (called a power of attorney).

auctor in rem suam one who acts in his own interest. Trustees and agents, for example, must not promote their own interests when handling others' affairs.

audi alteram partem hear the other side: the rule of natural justice that no decision should be reached by a court or tribunal until all parties have been given an opportunity to be heard.

Auditor of Court the court officer or other person responsible for the assessment of lawyers' fees in the Court of Session or sheriff court.

authority a judicial decision, authoritative textbook or statute justifying a proposition or statement of law.

avizandum the judge needs time to consider his verdict and prepare a judgement.

back bond or back letter an agreement in the form of a letter, qualifying the provisions of another document, for example agreeing that settlement of a loan payable on demand will not actually be demanded for a minimum of a year.

bairns' part the part of the moveable assets (cash, insurance policies, etc.) of a deceased person to which his children have a legal right despite the terms of any will. See **legitim**.

beneficiary a person who will benefit from the terms of a deed such as a will.

blood relationship the relationship between two people who have either one common parent (relationship of the half blood) or two common parents (relationship of the whole blood), as distinguished from relationship by marriage, where no parent is shared.

bona fide(s) (in) good faith.

bounding charter or **bounding title** a deed which defines the land comprised in it by reference to its boundaries. Reference may be to walls, roads or the land of another person, or by measurement.

brevitatis causa for the sake of brevity: a phrase incorporating by reference the terms of some other document, usually into writing.

brocard a legal maxim derived from Roman law or ancient

268

custom and regarded as part of the common law.

casus improvisus a situation not provided for or not foreseen, usually in the interpretation of rules, contracts and Acts of Parliament.

casus omissus a situation omitted, that should have been provided for within the existing law, especially in statute.

causa sine qua non the cause but for which the harm would not have resulted.

caveat a formal notice to a court requesting that warning be given to a party of the lodging of any case which seeks interim orders (e.g. interdict) against him and that such orders should not be granted until he has been able to appear before the court to oppose them.

citation (1) the procedure whereby a defender is called to court to answer an action or a witness to give evidence; (2) a reference to a previous case or opinion in support of a legal argument, i.e. where to find it published.

closed record the final written pleadings of the parties to a civil action.

codicil an addition to or alteration of a will without re-writing it entirely.

cognate a person related on the mother's side; the opposite of **agnate** (related on the father's side).

cognitionis causa tantum have the amount of the debt ascertained; an action raised by the creditor of a deceased debtor for the purpose of proving his debt to make a claim in the administration of the deceased's assets.

collateral security an additional security reinforcing the primary security for the performance of an obligation.

common debtor a debtor in respect of whom several creditors claim a share of arrested goods or money.

common interest an interest other than ownership which justifies a party exercising some control in the use of the property, for example a mutual wall between two houses.

common law law which does not derive from Acts of Parliament, etc. It includes law as laid down in judicial decisions and academic opinions.

composition an arrangement between a debtor and his creditors whereby debts are discharged in exchange for only an agreed partial payment.

confirmation (1) the authority of the court to an executor of a deceased person's estate to begin gathering in and administering the assets; (2) the document evidencing this authority.

conjoined arrestment order an order against the earnings of a debtor to enforce the payment to different creditors. Each creditor gets a share but the total deducted from the earnings each week or month is the same.

conjunct or confident persons persons closely related by blood or affinity, including business associates; transfer of assets to such persons is viewed suspiciously by creditors, especially in bankruptcies.

consensus in idem agreement as to those matters in a contract which are essential to make the contract binding, for example there is no consensus if one party believes he is hiring from another but the other believes he is selling to the first party.

contra proferentem against the person putting it forward. An ambiguous term in a contract will be read so as not to benefit the person who inserted it.

contributory negligence Since 1945 the court may reduce an award of damages in proportion to the claimant's share of responsibility for what happened.

counterclaim a claim by a defender in a case against the pursuer even though he could have sued for it separately if he wished.

creditor a person who is owed money.

curator ad litem a person appointed by the court to act for another person under disability (e.g. by reason of illness or mental disorder) whose interests have to be safeguarded in legal proceedings.

curator bonis a person appointed to act generally for a person incapable (through illness or absence) of administering his own affairs.

curatory the assets administered by a curator.

damages a sum of money claimed as compensation for loss or injury through negligence or breach of contract.

de facto in fact but not recognised by law, for example a *de facto* (but illegal) President.

de jure in law (but not necessarily in fact), for example a *de jure* (but exiled) President.

de minimis non curat lex the law does not concern itself with trifles; the courts will not provide a remedy for a trivial complaint.

de novo new, afresh; starting again from the beginning.

de plano summarily; without further legal enquiry; usually 'decree *de plano*'.

de presenti now, at the present time.

de recenti recent. Possession *de recenti* of stolen goods may create the presumption that the possessor is the thief.

decree the judgement of a court or arbiter in civil proceedings.

del credere agent describes an agreement by an agent to guarantee the performance by a third person in a contract to his employer.

delectus personae the choice of a specific person because of personal considerations. Such a person must perform a contract himself or be regarded as in breach of it.

delegatus non potest delegare a person entrusted with a task may not pass it on to someone else; or at least he will remain legally liable for loss whoever does the work.

delict negligent acts causing loss; the English term is tort.

dictum an opinion on a specific issue made by a judge in the course of a judgement.

dies non a day (e.g. a Sunday or public holiday) when judicial proceedings are not conducted.

dilatory defence a defence in civil proceedings designed to delay them; one without real substance.

dispone to transfer land.

disposition a formal deed transferring land.

docket or docquet an authenticating endorsement on a deed or other document, for example by a clerk of court to certify a true copy.

domicile the place where a person is considered by law to have his permanent home.

dominus litis the master of the litigation: usually refers to a party controlling a court case which has been raised in the name of someone else.

eadem persona cum defuncto the same person as the deceased. An executor is deemed to stand in the shoes of the deceased and is liable for the debts of the deceased but only to the value of the assets he controls.

edictal citation the **citation** of a person subject to the court's jurisdiction but outside Scotland or whose whereabouts are unknown, by delivery to a court official who enters it into a special register.

eik (pronounced 'eek') additional inventory of property not included in the original inventory of a deceased estate.

ejusdem generis of the same kind or class .

esto a technical terms used in written **pleadings** used to introduce a secondary line of defence which accepts, only for the sake of argument, facts which are still disputed in the primary defence, for example '*Esto* there was a contract (which is denied) the work was defective …'.

ex adverso opposite to; describing the position of land or buildings.

ex facie on the face of it. Something ex facie valid is presumed to be so unless contradicted by evidence.

ex gratia out of goodwill; an ex gratia payment may be made to settle a claim without any admission of liability.

ex lege according to law. Interest on money lent may be due to the creditor ex lege even if there was no specific agreement between the parties as to interest.

ex officio an office held by virtue of holding another office. Thus a Lord Provost may be ex officio a trustee of his city's Art Galleries Trust.

ex parte from one side; proceedings where only one party has had the opportunity of being heard.

ex post facto after the event.

ex proprio motu of his own accord: a decision made by a judge without a party requesting it.

excambion the exchange of one piece of land for another.

execution (1) the carrying out or enforcement of an order or decree of court; (2) certificate by a court officer that the court's order has been carried out; (3) the act of authenticating a deed by signing it in accordance with the appropriate formalities.

executor a legal representative of a deceased person whose duty is to administer the deceased's estate and implement the terms of any will.

executor dative an executor appointed by the sheriff where there is no will or the executors nominated decline to act or may be deceased themselves.

executor nominate an executor appointed by the deceased in terms of a will.

executry the process of winding up the estate of a deceased person in accordance with a will or with the law of **intestate** succession.

exoner to release from further liability, for example to allow a trustee to resign.

extract a formal copy of a decree or other judicial or legal document.

factor a person who manages property on behalf of the owner.

fatal accident inquiry an inquiry, conducted by the sheriff and initiated by the procurator fiscal, into any death which was sudden, suspicious or unexplained, or which occurred in circumstances giving rise to serious public concern.

feu a piece of land held by a feuar or vassal. Feudal land has conditions attached in favour of the superior (or ultimate owner), for example payment of feu duty. This is soon to be abolished by the Scottish Parliament.

fiduciary (1) (n.) a person who holds something in trust (in contrast to a beneficiary), and who must not use his position to derive an unauthorised profit or advantage for himself; (2) (n.) property held in trust; (3) (adj.) of the nature of a trust; held or given in trust.

filius nullius a bastard; this status is now relevant to the hereditary aristocracy only.

force majeure something beyond the control of ordinary parties to a contract, preventing its performance, for example a change in government regulations.

forum non conveniens a court or tribunal which is not appropriate, even though it may have jurisdiction, for example because all the witnesses may be in another area.

furthcoming an action to order a third party to pay arrested money to the creditor. See **arrestment**.

General Register of Sasines a public register, maintained since 1672, in which all deeds relating to land must be recorded. The register is gradually being superseded by the Land Register of Scotland but both have the same basic function.

grant (1) (n.) a deed transferring property; (2) (verb) to convey or transfer property to another.

grantee one to whom a grant is made.

granter one who makes a grant.

gratuitous without payment or other consideration, as opposed to **onerous**.

gratuitous alienation a transfer of property for no, or an inadequate, price, usually to the prejudice of someone's creditors.

habile admissible; valid; competent for a legal purpose.

habili modo in the manner competent. Thus a proof habili modo is a hearing where evidence will heard in a manner appropriate to the circumstances.

heritable property property consisting of land or buildings.

honorarium a form of financial gift as an acknowledgement for services, for example the secretary of a golf club.

hypothec a form of security over the property of a debtor but where the property is still in use by the debtor. This differs from pledge (as with a pawnbroker) where the goods are held and only given back if the debt is repaid. Thus a landlord has a hypothec for rent over his tenant's goods in the rented property.

in absentia in absence; undefended.

in camera proceedings heard in private, as distinct from in open court.

in causa in the case.

in flagrante delicto or *in flagrante crimine* in the very act of committing a wrong or crime.

in foro where an appearance or a defence has been entered; the opposite of **in absentia**.

in gremio in the body of; for example, any clause or words contained in a deed or document.

in hoc statu in this position, a phrase which makes it clear that something is being decided only in the light of the facts as known at the time, and can be re-opened.

in loco parentis in the place of a parent.

in meditatione fugae about to flee; usually describes a debtor:

the term is used to justify a court order to freeze his assets.

in rixa in the course of a quarrel. Objectionable words so spoken may not be actionable.

in solidum for the whole. Joint debtors bound *in solidum* are each liable to the creditor for full payment or performance, and the creditor may choose which debtor to sue.

in toto wholly; entirely.

incapax (1) (adj.) not capable; having legal, mental or physical incapacity; (2) (n.) a person who is *incapax*.

incorporeal describes property or rights which have no physical existence, for example an annuity or copyright.

induciae a period of time allowed in legal proceedings for a person to perform some act, for example for a defender to lodge notice of his intention to defend.

inhibition an order by the Court of Session, forbidding a debtor to sell or borrow money on security of his land, to the prejudice of a creditor.

injuria damage or loss.

inter partes between parties; each party is present or represented. Compare *ex parte*.

inter se between two or more persons or things.

inter vivos between living persons: describes deeds or legal acts intended to take effect during the granter's lifetime. Compare *mortis causa*.

interdict an order prohibiting an act or course of action (in England, an injunction);

interlocutor an order or judgement pronounced by the court in the course of a civil action. The final interlocutor is the decree.

intestate (1) (n.) a person who dies without having left a valid will; (2) (adj.) describes such a person or his estate.

invecta et illata the furniture, etc. of a tenant brought on to leased premises which are subject to the landlord's **hypothec** as security for rent.

ipso facto by the fact itself.

ipso jure by operation of law.

ish the date of termination or expiry of a lease.

joint and several obligation an obligation resting upon more than one person in which each obligant is liable for performance jointly or collectively with the others but also severally or individually. The creditor in such an obligation may sue all, or alternatively any one, of his debtors.

judgement the final determination in a litigation in which the judge sets forth his decision and, usually, his reasons for reaching it. See **decree** and **interlocutor**.

judicial factor a person appointed by a court to hold or administer property in Scotland where it is in dispute or where there is no one who could properly control or administer it. A judicial factor must have indemnity insurance and his work is supervised by the **Accountant of Court**.

judicial review a procedure in the Court of Session to review grievances by persons who allege that (i) decisions of inferior courts,public bodies,tribunals or other authorities (where no other form of appeal is provided) were outwith their powers or not in accordance with proper procedures or (ii) that such parties have failed to perform their duties in a proper manner. The Child Support Agency is an example of an organisation subject to judicial review.

jurisdiction (1) the authority of a court to hear and decide a particular case, an authority which may be restricted by territorial boundaries, the value or type of case or considerations, and which, in civil proceedings, is now determined primarily by European rules set out in the Civil Jurisdiction and Judgements Act 1982; (2) the territorial area within which a particular court may exercise that authority.

jus relictae the right of the widow to claim against her husband's estate even if she was left out of his will. A widower has a similar right, the *jus relicti*.

lacuna (1) an omission or blank space in a document; (2) a situation not covered by rules or regulations when it should have been.

legitim a child's right to claim against a deceased parent's estate even if they were left out of the parent's will.

lex contractus the law to be applied to a contract. This may not be the same as the law of the place where the contract was performed, because the parties may have agreed otherwise.

lex domicilii the law of the domicile. The law of someone's domicile or the law of his nationality. See also **domicile**.

lex fori the law of the court; the law of the country in which litigation takes place, and which regulates matters such as evidence and court procedure

lex loci actus the law of the place where the act was performed.

lex loci contractus the law of the place where the contract was made or concluded. This law may be the same as the law of the contract itself but where different governs formal matters such as capacity, for example what age parties have to be to enter into a contract.

lex loci delicti the law of the place where a negligent act was committed.

lex loci rei sitae the law of the place where the subject of the action (usually land) is situated.

lien (pronounced 'lee-en') a right to retain a debtor's moveable property until he has paid his debt.

limitation period the period within which an action or claim must be raised in court. If an action is raised out of time the claim will usually be barred from proceedings.

liquid debt a debt or claim of an known amount which is legally overdue.

liquidate damages damages stipulated in a contract without proof of actual loss, for example £500 per week for delay beyond the completion date for building a house.

liquidation the procedure for winding up a limited company; the equivalent of an individual's bankruptcy.

lis alibi pendens a case pending elsewhere: a defence that the same question as that raised in the present action is already the subject of litigation in another court.

litiscontestation the stage at which a court action becomes contested.

locum tenens a person who acts as substitute or depute for another, for example a doctor.

locus delicti the place where the delict or crime was committed.

locus standi a place to stand: the right to be heard by a court or tribunal.

mala fide(s) in bad faith; lacking good faith.

man of skill an expert to whom a court may remit a technical matter before it for investigation and report.

mens rea guilty purpose or criminal intent.

misfeasance the wrongful or unlawful performance of official duty.

missives the letters exchanged by the parties which constitute a binding contract to buy and sell land, setting forth the terms and conditions in detail.

mortis causa in contemplation of death.

multiplepoinding (pronounced 'multiplepinding') an action in which the court is asked to adjudicate upon conflicting claims made to property or money held by a third party, for example the police holding stolen property with more than one person claiming to be the rightful owner.

mutatis mutandis making the necessary alterations. An existing document used for another purpose is read as altered to meet the different circumstances, for example trout could be bought using a salmon contract if it were to be read *mutatis mutandis*.

nexus bond, or relationship by legal acts, for example a contract creates a nexus between the parties.

nimious excessive.

nomen juris legal term: any word having a particular technical legal meaning, for example 'delict'.

non compos mentis of unsound mind.

non sequitur an illogical conclusion.

notary public an official before whom affidavits and other documents may be sworn.

novation holding an obligation (e.g. a debt) to be at an end by replacing it with a new one, with the consent of all the parties concerned.

obiter dictum an opinion expressed by a judge on a point which is not essential to the decision of the case before him. Such opinions are not binding on other judges.

obtemper to obey, comply with or fulfil, used especially of a court order.

onerous given for value, payment or services, as opposed to **gratuitous**.

onus of proof (*onus probandi*) the burden of proving each disputed issue of fact arising in a litigation.

ostensible usually seen in the phrase 'ostensible authority'; reliance placed by others on the authority of someone to enter into contracts on behalf of another person he certainly appears to represent.

paction an agreement or contract.

pari passu equally; taking the same share or priority, usually when dividing up a debtor's assets.

parts and pertinents everything which passes with the actual land on its transfer or disposition, for example minerals or fishing rights.

passing off the misrepresentation of a business or goods with the purpose or effect of misleading the public into thinking that the business or the goods are those of another.

pendente lite so long as an action is pending before a court.

per incuriam through mistake or error, for example something omitted from a deed.

periculo petentis at the risk of the perpetrator. Thus if a bank account were arrested in error, the creditor would be liable in damages.

personal bar the rule precluding a person from raising in court issues which his opponent believes were already resolved, provided that the opponent has done something to his disadvantage in relying on the previous arrangement, for example accepting a cheque in full and final settlement.

pleadings the formal written presentation of a party's case in court in a civil action.

plenishing furniture, equipment, stock or gear.

poind (pronounced 'pind') – to seize a debtor's goods in his possession and inventory them prior to their public sale or handing over to the creditor in satisfaction of a decree.

post litem motam after an action has been raised.

precognition a preliminary statement of the evidence which a witness may be expected to give, taken down in writing. It is not signed and cannot usually be produced in court.

prescription rules of law by which rights are gained or lost by lapse of time, for example establishing a right of way or failing to sue for damages.

prima facie at first appearance or sight. A *prima facie* case is one which, at first sight, appears compelling and calls for an answer.

primo loco in the first place. *Secundo loco* means in the second place, and so forth.

pro bono publico for the public good; for the advantage of the public generally.

pro indiviso in common; in an undivided manner; as of one person's right in property owned in common by two or more persons.

pro non scripto as if not written; matters in a deed that are ignored, for example illegal or impossible conditions in a will.

pro rata proportionately.

probabilis causa litigandi a probable or plausible ground of action, for example an applicant for legal aid must demonstrate that he has such grounds for taking or defending the proceedings in question.

probation proof of facts in civil proceedings.

production a document or article produced as evidence in court (in English law, an exhibit).

prorogate (1) to confer on a court, by consent of the parties, jurisdiction to hear a case it could not otherwise allow to proceed; (2) to extend a time limit for procedure in the course of a litigation.

proving the tenor an action in which the pursuer seeks to prove, from drafts, copies or otherwise, the contents of a lost or destroyed document.

quantum how much, for example damages payable.

quantum lucratus how much gained; where work has been done with no agreement at all (say a garage built on a neighbour's driveway instead of yours) the person who has gained will have to pay the builder but only by the amount his house has increased in value, which may not be the same as the cost of the works themselves. Compare *quantum meruit*.

quantum meruit what it is worth. Where parties agreed that work was to be done but did not agree a price then the contractor is entitled to the going rate, as opposed to *quantum lucratus*.

quantum valeat for what it is worth; a court may allow what appears to be irrelevant evidence to be led, just in case it sheds light on the case later.

quid pro quo something given in return for something else; the price paid for goods.

quoad ultra all the rest; in civil actions some of the facts may be admitted and quoad ultra denied.

ratio decidendi the judge's legal reason or ground on which a case is decided.

rebut to counter an opponent's case with evidence or arguments.

reclaim to appeal in a defended action.

repetition the repayment of money which has been paid in error.

repone to appeal in an undefended action.

repudiate to indicate by actions or words that a party does not intend to perform an obligation.

res judicata a case or issue decided finally, so that it may not be raised again in a litigation between the same parties.

res nullius something which belongs to nobody.

res sua one's own property.

rescind to terminate or cancel a contract for lawful reasons, as opposed to merely breaking it.

restitutio in integrum entire restoration: putting someone back in the position in which they would have been had the transaction or event in question not taken place.

retrocession the opposite of assignation; giving back a right conveyed to another, most commonly an insurance policy assigned as additional security for a house loan.

separatim separately; a technical term of written pleadings introducing a secondary line of defence which is unrelated to the principal defence, for example a **counterclaim**.

sine die indefinitely; without a day being fixed, for example for a resumption of adjourned proceedings.

sine qua non an essential condition or factor.

solatium compensation or damages given for the injury to feelings, reputation, pain, suffering and loss of expectation of life, as opposed to, say, loss of earnings.

sponsiones ludicrae a promise in jest; an agreement unenforceable because the parties did not seriously intend to be bound in law, for example a bet.

sub judice in the hands of the law; a matter or dispute pending before a court: this usually means that it cannot be discussed or commented upon until the case is over.

subrogation the legal principle under which a person who has paid money to someone is entitled to take up any right to recover what he paid from a third party, for example a motor insurance company, having paid out to its policyholder, can still sue the other driver if they caused the accident.

suo periculo at one's own risk.

survivorship clause a clause in a will or conveyance which provides that should one of the several beneficiaries or grantees die before they inherit, their interest is to pass to the survivor or those who survive.

taciturnity a presumption that the inactivity of a creditor means that the obligation is no longer due.

tantum et tale something accepted by a buyer just as it is, without warranty.

taxation the assessment of a solicitor's account for legal expenses or charges in litigation by the Auditor of Court to establish a fair fee.

terminus a quo the point from which a time limit begins to run.

testate having died leaving a valid will.

testing clause the clause at the end of a deed identifying the arties signing and specifying the date and place of **execution** and the witnesses' details.

time bar the effect of lapse of time on a person's rights, preventing them from taking steps to enforce those rights or extinguishing them entirely. See also **prescription**.

timeous within the period allowed by law.

title to sue legal right to raise an action.

toties quoties as often as; for each time.

uberrimae fidei in utmost good faith; having concealed nothing.

ultimus haeres the ultimate heir. The Crown is *ultimus haeres* if there are no other heirs.

ultra vires beyond the powers. The term is used especially in the context of local government, trustees and companies who purport to have the authority to do something but legally they do not.

unjust enrichment the principle that a person who receives an unmerited and unjustifiable benefit to another person's loss should recompense that other person. See *quantum lucratus*.

unum quid one thing; where several things are for some purpose or reason considered and treated together as one.

vacant possession no obstruction and no person (such as a tenant) in occupation to prevent a purchaser enjoying actual possession of a property.

verba jacantia empty, vain words; words spoken in jest.

vergens ad inopiam on the brink of becoming insolvent.

vexatious litigant a person who brings proceedings primarily for the purpose of annoying or embarrassing the defender. The Court of Session may prohibit a vexatious litigant from raising court actions unless the court's approval has first been obtained.

vi *clam aut precario* to hold by force, or otherwise without legal right, for example a squatter.

vitious intromitter a person who takes possession of the property of a deceased person without lawful authority.

void null; having no legal effect whatsoever, for example a marriage by a person under age.

voidable apparently valid, but tainted in some way, so that a contract, deed or obligation may be declared invalid at a later date but remains in force until then.

waiver an express or implied voluntary renunciation of a right. A superior may expressly renounce or modify conditions in a feu charter by a minute of waiver.

warrant a written judicial authority, for example for service of a writ, sale, search or eviction.

warrant sale the public sale of articles which have been **poinded**.

warranty an express or implied material guarantee in a contract.

winding up the process of liquidation or bringing to a close the affairs of a limited company which has become insolvent.

without prejudice (1) in statutes or documents, this phrase introduces a saving clause, creating an exception to the provision in which the phrase is used;
(2) in negotiations for the settlement of a dispute, indicates correspondence which, if the negotiations fail, is not to be founded on in later litigation.

wrongous wrongful, for example 'wrongous imprisonment'.